Hardcover Out of Print

10ⁿ⁵

HOW TO BE
TWICE AS SMART

Boosting Your
Brainpower and
Unleashing the Miracles
of Your Mind

Other Books by the Author

Automatic Wealth-Building Formulas That Pile Up Riches Fast

Control Dynamics for Mastery Over People

How Self-Made Millionaires Build Their Fortunes

How to Make Big Money at Home in Your Spare Time

Spare-Time Businesses You Can Start and Run with Less Than $1,500

HOW TO BE TWICE AS SMART

Boosting Your Brainpower and Unleashing the Miracles of Your Mind

Scott Witt

PARKER PUBLISHING COMPANY, INC.
WEST NYACK, NEW YORK

© 1983 by

PARKER PUBLISHING COMPANY, INC.
West Nyack, NY

Library of Congress Cataloging in Publication Data

Witt, Scott
How to be twice as smart.

Includes index.
1. Intellect.   2. Thought and thinking.
3. Learning, Psychology of.   4. Success.   I. Title.
BF431.W582   1983   153   82-14358
ISBN 0-13-402347-1
ISBN 0-13-402339-0 {PBK}

Printed in the United States of America

Introduction

Most people use ten percent or less of their brainpower, leaving a vast reserve of mental ability unused. This book reveals how to tap that idle brainpower and double your mental performance. By making fuller use of the potential you already have, you will improve your:

* Memory
* Reading efficiency
* Math ability
* Problem-solving talent
* Learning speed
* Creativity
* Relationships with other people
* Writing skills
* Prowess for outsmarting competitors

To say that you can double your performance in these areas is an understatement. Actually, you can do much better; but doubling is a good start. Let's take a closer look at some of the accomplishments you can expect with the help of Mental Leverage.

DEVELOP A TOTAL RECALL MEMORY

Your memory is one of your most important assets, but until you learn the techniques spelled out in this book, you're not making it really perform for you.

There is no need to forget people's names now that the Linkage Technique makes total name recall a snap. There's no need to have important facts slip by you when the Data Indexing Method gives you instant access to them. Figures and dates? They're a breeze when you use Digit Conversions.

FASTER READING MADE EASY

You won't learn speed reading in this book. You'll pick up something much better: High-Performance Reading. Being able to zip through the pages isn't the only benefit. You'll also absorb much more.

WHO NEEDS A CALCULATOR?

The first thing you're going to do when it comes to math is forget almost everything you ever learned about numbers. Then you're going to pick up exciting new methods that have you adding and subtracting columns of figures as fast as if you had a calculator—perhaps even faster. Multiplying and dividing is just as quick with this new method.

SOLVE THE UNSOLVABLE

When we talk about solving problems in this book, we're talking about the real toughies—the mind benders that would have been unsolvable without the techniques spelled out here. You're going to tap your mind's most hidden resource—your subconscious—and use it to get great solutions other people would never dream of.

BECOME A SPEED LEARNER

Most people spend far too much time studying, not realizing that they should be speed learning instead. You'll see how it's done using such secrets as Mental Activation, Total Involvement, and Programmed Learning.

DEVELOP INGENIOUS NEW IDEAS

There is a lot of creative genius in your mind, just as there's a lot in everybody's mind. Unfortunately, most people don't know how to unlock it. You're about to learn some unique methods that unlock your creative genius by utilizing your ingenuity, curiosity, and subconscious.

A GREAT METHOD FOR CREATING IDEAS AND SOLUTIONS

So powerful is this one method of originating dynamic ideas that an entire chapter is devoted to it. You'll find it fascinating and fun when you begin Wildcatting for the ideas and solutions that you need. You'll also become a much more productive person in your job or business because you'll always have figured out how to do things the easy way.

GAIN A DEEPER UNDERSTANDING

You have a lot to gain by learning how to obtain important information that other people miss. For example: decoding hidden meanings, getting information from people who don't want to give it to you, and understanding interpersonal signals. These are all Mental Leverage skills that you can easily acquire.

PEOPLE POWER: THE ULTIMATE MENTAL ABILITY

A successful person needs more than brainpower; he also needs people-power—the ability to get others to agree with him and do as he bids. Learn verbal techniques that give you instant mastery over others, and you've got a major key to success. Discover how to resolve disagreements to your own benefit and how to impress the people who can help you most. It's all here.

HOW TO MOTIVATE PEOPLE WITH WHAT YOU WRITE

Whether it's a letter, memo, report, or résumé, the object is to get others to read it carefully and take the action it calls for. Can you truthfully say that most of what you write commands that type of response? There is a system that uses the written word to get what you want—and I'm going to share it with you.

USE SIMULATION TECHNIQUES TO BUILD SUPER-PERFORMANCE

Individuals can now latch on to one of the most sophisticated learning methods developed by science, industry, and government. However, you don't need the gadgetry they use. You'll discover how a simple $2 purchase can give you a learning experience that compares with a $250,000 training machine, and how one company actually opted for the $2 alternative. What worked well for them will do even better for you.

DRAW ON A WEALTH OF WISDOM

As fabulous as your mind is, it can never equal the knowledge and genius that reside in many minds put together. If two heads are better than one, just think what a dozen or more can do. That's the benefit of Personal Networking—today's newest method for giving private individuals access to the world's best brains. You'll find full details on joining a network that can make a huge change in your life.

PUT MENTAL LEVERAGE TO WORK FOR YOU

The super-performers of this world got where they are not because they are any smarter than the rest of us, but because they know how to leverage their brainpower. When you begin using this same type of leverage, you'll see immediate results. Thanks to Mental Leverage you can:

* Get your paperwork done in half the time
* Remember the names of everyone you meet
* Recall facts, dates, and figures from your encyclopedic memory
* Do mental calculations at the speed of a calculator
* Read a complete book in less time than most people take for one chapter
* Solve problems that stump others
* Impress the people who can help you most
* Set higher goals for yourself and meet them easily

The key to all of these achievements is Mental Leverage, and it's spelled out for you, step by step, in the pages and chapters of this book.

Scott Witt

Contents

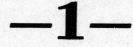

How to Cash in on Your Unused Brainpower

We owe a lot to the inventors and scientists who have done so much to make our lives better. It's too bad they've failed in one major area. Physically, they've achieved wonders, giving us machines that cook our meals or transport our bodies in a fraction of the time it used to take. But so far they haven't come up with anything to improve our minds.

Yes, there are computers that will play chess with you and calculators that will give you a square root in less than a second, but what about the everyday learning, remembering, and problem solving each of us has to do? When you are considered for a job or promotion, the interviewer is interested in what *you* can do, not your calculator.

You'll be pleased to learn that even without any help from the scientists and inventors, you can do very well, indeed. In fact, you can do much better than you are now doing, regardless of your present level of achievement.

PROVEN TECHNIQUES FOR SHARPENING YOUR MENTAL POWERS

If this is your first exposure to the system known as Mental Leverage, you're in for a pleasant surprise. You're about to discover an exciting new way to:

1

* Sharpen your memory.
* Learn more rapidly.
* Read faster and retain more.
* Handle math much easier.
* Quickly solve different problems.
* Increase your creativity.
* Wield more control over other people.
* Gain a deeper understanding of what you read and hear.
* Become a better-informed person.

THE NEW MEANING OF LEVERAGE

Mental Leverage is a lot like the other forms of leverage you've been using all your life. With the aid of a physical lever, your muscles can move objects they would never budge otherwise. Financial leverage allows you to use a relatively small amount of money as a down payment on the purchase of something expensive, like a home, car, or business. In these forms of leverage, what counts is not how many muscles or dollars you've got—but where and how you apply them.

It's the same with Mental Leverage. It's not how much thinking, or studying, or memorizing you do—it's the way you go about it. This book reveals proven methods for leveraging your brainpower with techniques employed by many of today's top achievers. They've utilized its wonders to:

* Qualify for better jobs and higher pay
* Build successful businesses
* Achieve new sales records
* Control difficult people
* Forge ahead in politics
* Become recognized experts in a variety of fields

People who haven't learned how to use Mental Leverage often find it difficult to remember needed information, and they must struggle to solve many kinds of problems. They impose needless limitations on themselves, their careers, and their relationships with others. They fail to realize how great their mental potential really is.

MIND IS THE GREAT LEVER OF ALL THINGS

Many of the techniques of Mental Leverage are well known to people who have achieved outstanding success in business. And why not? Experience has taught them the underlying principle. They have learned the power of leverage in financing their enterprises, repeatedly making one dollar do the work of ten or more.

Early in their careers they realize that their potential for success is limited only by their own creativity and problem-solving ability. So, agreeing with Daniel Webster that "mind is the great lever of all things," they vow to multiply their mental power in much the same way they've been leveraging their financial power.

Many of the techniques in this book are based on the individual "levers" these leaders have developed. Just as you will, these businessmen and businesswomen have concentrated on the areas where they needed the most strength. While a salesman might need to improve his memory of names, products, and prices, the head of an electronics firm might need to triple his or her reading speed in order to keep up with the latest developments. And both of them might benefit greatly from unlocking their creative abilities in order to come up with exciting new business ideas.

Out of necessity, the real achievers in the business world have developed highly effective methods for getting the brain performance they need and demand. You'll find the best of their methods in this book.

HOW TO OUTSMART PEOPLE WITH TWICE YOUR IQ

The law of averages says that if you were to sit down and take an intelligence test with a bunch of other people, some of them would obtain higher scores than you. But don't let it bother you, because when it comes to real life situations, you can beat any of them. Here's why:

1. Nobody functions at a level anywhere near his or her mental capacity.

2. All you have to do to outperform someone else—even if that person is "smarter" than you—is to increase your own Mental Performance Ratio.

Your Mental Performance Ratio (MPR) is simply the percentage of your total mental capacity that you are putting to use. If you're like most people, you're using only about ten percent of your brainpower. But when you apply Mental Leverage, your mind performs as if the percentage were much greater.

If, for example, your memory normally functions at ten percent of capacity, the Mental Leverage techniques you apply for improving your memory allow you to perform as if your Mental Performance Ratio were well above ten percent. When you double your ability to recall facts and figures (as many people do with Mental Leverage) your MPR is effectively twenty percent instead of ten percent. The person who beat you in the IQ test is still functioning at ten percent, and with your use of Mental Leverage, you can outperform him hands down.

Let's be conservative. Let's say that instead of doubling your capacity, you've only increased it by one-fifth. For the sake of our example, we'll deal with learning. You have increased your ability to learn new material by one-fifth. Thus, your MPR for learning is twelve percent instead of ten percent.

Now let's say that John Jones has an IQ of 140, while yours is 120. Under normal conditions, he should be able to learn faster than you. But these aren't normal conditions, because you are applying Mental Leverage to the learning process. This makes you "smarter" than Mr. Jones. Simple arithmetic explains why.

YOU:	IQ rating	120
	Your MPR	×.12
	Your learning power	14.4
JOHN JONES:	IQ rating	140
	His MPR	×.10
	Jones' learning power	14.0

Your learning power is now above that of John Jones. You can easily outperform him.

THE COMPETITIVE EDGE THAT BRINGS SUCCESS

The senior vice president in charge of personnel at a major New York City bank wrote me not long ago after having read an article of mine on MPR. The article explained that even a slight improvement in your Mental Performance Ratio can have a big impact on your career. Here's what the bank executive wrote:

> The article was of particular interest to me because I am living proof that what you say is true. Being in charge of personnel here at the bank, I have access to all of the employment records. The other day I happened across the file of a high school chum of mine. Irv and I both joined the bank the same year. The records show that he and I got identical scores on the aptitude test that was administered prior to our being hired.
>
> Irv and I were quite close during our first years at the bank. Living in the same town, we commuted together. Both of us were highly ambitious. Irv was always taking papers home to work on at night or on weekends. I took a different tack. Instead of using my free time to do the bank's work, I decided to devote some time to increasing my mental skills. That way, I figured, I could improve my performance on the job, turning in more and better work during the eight hours I was at my desk.
>
> The time Irv spent doing bank work at home did, of course, help solve some immediate problems—but it had no long-lasting impact on the bank or his career. There was always another pile of work to be done the next day. On the other hand, the time I spent learning to read faster, solve problems easier, and improve my memory, has paid dividends throughout the years. My ability to perform better and faster was noticed, and I was singled out for a steady stream of promotions.
>
> Irv, too, was noticed. His superiors appreciated the work done on his own time, and he, too, received some promotions. But now, as I look back on it, I realize the big difference in how the bank recognized the two of us. Irv had gained a reputation merely as a hard worker. My

reputation, on the other hand, was and is that of an unusually bright man and a highly skilled banker.

The aptitude test scores I ran across the other day show I'm no more intelligent than Irv. I merely learned how to apply my intelligence in more effective ways. Until reading your article, Mr. Witt, I'd never heard the term "Mental Performance Ratio" but now I know that improving my own MPR is what caused my career to zoom.

It's why I'm now a senior vice president, and Irv is in the junior officer ranks. He's working just as hard as ever, still taking papers home. He continues to be a friend of mine, and out of friendship I plan on showing him your article.

As his letter states, this bank executive became able to accomplish much more in his eight hours on the job than his friend could do in eight hours-plus-homework. His superiors noticed his sharper mental skills and he was promoted far more rapidly.

You are in an even better position than our banker friend. He was on his own in sharpening his mental skills. You have this book as your complete guide to a rapid system of advancing your Mental Performance Ratio.

ISO-MENTAL EXERCISES THAT BUILD SHARP MINDS

You might think of the techniques in this book as isometric exercises for the brain. You know, of course, what isometric exercises are. They were discovered by a research scientist in Germany who was studying muscular action. One day he tied one leg of a frog to a table in his laboratory. The other leg was left untied. The frog, not realizing there was no way to free its tied leg, kept pushing it against the twine, which, of course, would not give.

It wasn't long before the research scientist made an important discovery. Extra-large muscles began to develop in the leg that was tied down—the leg whose muscles were repeatedly being contracted in pushing against an immovable object (the twine). Why not, the scientist wondered, use this same principle in developing human muscles? This is how isometric exercises were introduced.

People who want to develop arm muscles push their two hands against each other, with all the strength they can muster for a ten-second period. Those who desire flat stomachs suck them in as far as they can for a similar period. Legs are pushed up against table tops to make them muscular. Someone has even come up with isometric exercises for the face!

THE SECRET OF LEARNING FASTER AND REMEMBERING MORE

The success of isometrics stems from the fact that you are using your muscles to increase their own strength. You are exerting those muscles to their limit, pushing against an immovable force. This has a far greater effect than weight lifting for the same length of time. In weight lifting, the force may be heavy, but it's certainly not immovable. Because the weight gives way to the pressure of your muscles, they are getting less of a workout than if they pushed against something that cannot give.

The appeal of all this, of course, is that in just seconds a day a person can develop muscles that would take thirty minutes a day to develop with normal exercise routines.

Your ability to learn and remember can be developed in the same way. The secret of learning faster and remembering more is to give each of the mind-building techniques in this book a brief but regular workout. It should be done every day, just as the muscle-builder applies isometric techniques on a daily basis. As in isometrics, it takes only seconds for each exercise.

Consider these similarities between sharpening your mind with Mental Leverage and building your body with isometrics:

* A few minutes a day has the same effect as an hour or more of normal training.

* Your practice can be conducted while you are doing other things.

* Just as isometrics uses muscles to develop themselves, Mental Leverage uses your brain to make itself more powerful.

USE ODD MINUTES,
SPARE SECONDS FOR MIND BUILDING

Because he was probably only using ten percent of his mental powers, a friend of mine was not able to keep up-to-date in his job. Gene R. works in a highly technical field, and he was overwhelmed by all the new material he was expected to learn.

"It seems that every day there's a big pile of new data pushed on me," Gene complained, "and there just isn't enough time to read about it, let alone really get to understand it."

I asked Gene how he'd like to be able to double his reading speed.

"That would be great, if it were possible," he responded.

And how would he like to cut in half the time it takes to learn new material?

"That would be even better."

When I told Gene there were easy-to-master techniques that could greatly enhance his reading and learning speeds, his interest was aroused—but only for a moment. After he'd had time for a second thought, Gene said:

"I'm in such a mess, I can't spend any time studying new learning techniques or taking speed reading courses."

And then I explained to Gene what I've been telling you. Nearly all the techniques contained in this book can be developed in practice sessions that take just minutes per day. And much of the practice comes during the normal course of your day, while you're going about your regular business.

EASY MIND-STRETCHING EXERCISES

"Tell you what," I said to Gene, "let's have lunch together one day each week for the next several weeks. Each week I'll show you a new technique for speeding up your reading or comprehension. For the following seven days, you practice that technique. No need to take time out from your regular activities; you can work the practice in with whatever else you're doing. You can manage that, can't you?"

Gene agreed that he could. In our luncheon meetings, I revealed to him the techniques you'll be learning in Chapters 2,

3, and 6. Obviously, he didn't get the full benefits of Mental Leverage because there is a lot of valuable material that we never touched on. He needed a crash course to help him out of an overwhelming predicament, and that's what he got.

At our second meeting, I asked Gene how his first week's practice had gone.

"Great!" he replied, "I not only practiced what you taught me in those ten-second exercises you talked about, I actually put them to use in my job. And they work just fine!"

Within several weeks, Gene was well on his way out of his predicament. He was using exciting new methods for high-performance reading, and he was utilizing the basics of instant learning. He was no longer overwhelmed by the requirements of his job.

"In fact," Gene reported, "it has become almost a breeze. I'm keeping on top of things like never before."

Obviously, people around him noticed the change in his attitude and performance. Since learning those three elements of Mental Leverage, he's had two promotions. The techniques he's learned enabled him not only to do well in the work he had been doing, but to tackle additional responsibilities as well. He's been spotted as a real "comer" in his company.

THE POWER OF SPEED REASONING

Great as these attributes are, to be truly successful you must be more than a fast reader, a quick learner, or a good memorizer.

You'll gain each of these attributes as you progress in Mental Leverage, and they should do a wealth of good for you. But what about the problems that keep cropping up? Everyone is faced with daily problems of various magnitudes, and they can rob us of time and energy—even drain us emotionally. Most people spend so much time thinking and worrying about problems, there's little energy left to deal with them.

Speed Reasoning to the rescue. Speed Reasoning, as taught in this book, has you dealing instantly with important problems and getting them quickly out of the way. And this can work wonders in your life.

People who practice Speed Reasoning gain reputations as

decision makers. They're able to analyze a situation or problem almost at a glance, and quickly come up with the right decisions and solutions.

You read and hear a lot about the nation's decision makers—both in government and in the business world. You think of decision makers as people at the top, but the odds are that they were decision makers long before they reached the top.

During a break in a conference we were both attending, the chairman of a large corporation and I were discussing decision makers.

"It's like the chicken or the egg question," Jim said. "There's a lot of argument over whether top executives become agile decision makers before or after they become top executives. I believe that most top executives achieve their rank because of their decision-making ability. First they demonstrate that they know how to make the right decisions rapidly, and then they're rewarded with positions of increasing responsibility."

Jim says people who demonstrate decision-making ability early in their careers are quickly singled out for advancement, but he also notes that it's never too late to become known as a decision maker.

HOW SPEED REASONING RESHAPES CAREERS

I've heard Jim tell the story several times, and I've not tired of hearing it. I believe that you, too, know the benefits to be derived from learning how other people achieve outstanding success, so I've obtained Jim's permission to relate the experience here.

As Jim tells it, there was a middle-aged man in the company where he worked, a man who was frequently bypassed for promotion. "Younger men and women—people who'd been with the firm for far less time—were being promoted over him. In a number of cases, he found himself being an underling to people who had formerly worked under him.

"Sure, the fellow had a position of responsibility, but it was in the lower echelons of his company. He was a junior executive going nowhere. One day, while at lunch with a colleague, he wondered out loud why his career was dead-ended. And he was surprised at the answer voiced by his friend.

"The friend told him that although he had most of the qualifications for more important jobs within the company, he lacked one major qualification—decisiveness. The friend said, rather bluntly, that he had to stop going to superiors for advice and start making some key decisions on his own.

"His immediate reaction was to point out that he consulted superiors on major questions because they wanted him to. His friend explained that the reason they wanted to be consulted was that he had never demonstrated any bold decision-making ability on his own.

"Well, after thinking over what his friend had told him, he decided to do something about it. He read all he could on decision-making, problem-solving, and personal creativity. He devised his own curriculum for learning what is now known as Speed Reasoning. He found it's a skill that anyone can develop; it's not a talent you're born with.

"The upshot is that things began to change rapidly for this fellow. His bosses, even those younger than he, began to notice his new assertiveness. And since most of the decisions he was now making were right on target, they were highly impressed with his performance.

"At middle age, that man's career was given new impetus. He began receiving all the promotions that had bypassed him in earlier years. Now he was bypassing those who had risen above him.

"He was even being noticed by other companies in the same industry. Eventually, one of them hired him away—as chairman of the board, no less.

"Perhaps you've guessed who I'm talking about. I am the man whose life was changed in mid-career by Speed Reasoning."

Unlike Jim, you may not aspire to be chairman of the board, but I'm sure you'll agree that if it could be a major factor in his success, it can do the same in helping you achieve whatever your goals might be.

THE ELEMENTS OF SPEED REASONING

You won't find a chapter in this book with Speed Reasoning in its title. That's because there are a number of elements that go into Speed Reasoning. Thus, you'll pick up Speed Reasoning skills in several chapters, such as:

* Chapter 5, revealing an easy way to solve tough problems
* Chapter 7, helping you unlock your own creative genius
* Chapter 8, your source of dynamic ideas and powerful solutions
* Chapter 9, a guide to gaining valuable information others miss

Speed Reasoning is one of the most dynamic elements of success. Business firms have spent millions to have their executives trained in its elements, all of which you have here, for the price of this book.

But, just as orange juice isn't just for breakfast anymore, Speed Reasoning isn't just for business. People from all walks of life find it a valuable asset in:

* Making wiser decisions affecting their personal lives
* Dealing with problems that crop up suddenly
* Handling difficult people
* Becoming effective leaders in community and religious groups
* Becoming more adept at mind games such as chess and backgammon

HOW TO FREE YOUR CREATIVE GENIUS

No one can doubt that the human brain is the most awesome part of the body. It weighs just three pounds and it has often been described as a marvel of complexity and miniaturization. It is, in effect, an electrochemical computer. The information it receives, stores, and transmits is conveyed by means of an electrochemical network, in much the same way that electronic computers use wires and printed circuits to move their data around.

But no electronic computer—regardless of weight or size—has ever been devised to duplicate the wonders of the human brain. Throughout your lifetime, your brain has continuously received and stored information sent to it in the form of electrical signals by your eyes, ears, nose, fingers, and other sensory equipment. The billions of facts and impressions that have been sifted by your brain would fill an estimated ninety million books.

To continue the computer analogy, the human brain is a data processor, and one of its most marvelous abilities allows it to withdraw facts and impressions from its memory bank, put them together, and come up with something entirely new. When you're a child, this ability is called imagination. Adults prefer to call it creativity. In childhood, it's used for play; in adulthood, it's used to solve problems, launch fortunes, cure diseases, and win all kinds of contests and competitions.

PROGRAM YOURSELF FOR CREATIVITY

Many people believe that creativity is an inbred talent, and that if you weren't born with much of it, there's no way to develop more. The facts I've assembled prove otherwise. I've seen example after example in which people have "programmed" their minds to come up with creative solutions. The result, in many instances, has been a complete turnaround: people leading unimpressive, humdrum lives have utilized their newfound creativity to achieve sudden success.

Here are just a few examples of what has been done by what I call Programmed Creativity:

* A bank clerk devised a system to help prevent computer fraud in financial institutions and became a millionare.

* A housewife who was tired of moving every time her husband was transferred came up with a plan that convinced his company he was extremely valuable right where he was.

* A candidate for state senator was trailing in the polls until he began using his own creativity to attract the attention of the voters who then elected him to office.

* A secretary who knew she was really executive material was able to leave her typewriter behind after she conceived a creative method of getting her bosses to think of her as too talented for the steno pool.

* A man who was appointed chairman of the fund drive for the volunteer ambulance corps in his city devised a

highly creative fund-raising method that brought in more dollars than had been collected in any previous year. The success of the drive impressed many influential people, who took notice of him for the first time. The next year, he was appointed city manager at three times the salary he'd been receiving in the private sector. *

None of these people were the kind you'd think of as being particularly creative, yet they were able to come up with imaginative solutions that brought highly pleasing results. You'll be learning their technique in this book. Pay particular attention to Chapter 7.

A LESSON IN LEARNING

"It floored me," Howard V. recalls. "Grown men and women—colleagues of mine in the executive ranks of a large company—actually afraid of the boxes I had placed on their desks."

Howard's experience occurred after he began to implement what he had thought was a great idea. A lot of financial planning is done in his company, and the people involved in it had, for years, used charts, graphs, and spread sheets that cluttered their desks. They'd pore over figures hour after hour with pencil, eraser, and calculator.

"One day I read in a business magazine about a program written for small, personal computers that did in minutes what many financial executives were taking hours to do by hand. The program had taken the country by storm. It allowed you to set up financial spread sheets containing many rows and columns of figures. Then, in making plans for your company, you could change one or more of the figures; the result was that any other figures relating to those you had changed would automatically be changed as'well. Thus you could see what effect various factors might have on the future of your company.

"If, for example, you had based your projections on a nine percent annual inflation rate, but wanted to see what inflation of twelve percent would do to your company, just one or two entries on the keyboard would do it for you. Before this program was available, you'd have to manually recalculate scores of figures on your paper charts.

"Before putting computers on the desks of my financial planners, I decided to try one myself. I took it home for some weekend practice, and found the program worked fine and would be suitable for our needs. When I was through with the trial, I let my twelve-year-old son play with it. He took to computing right away and, in fact, quickly learned how to operate the financial planning program. He used it to convince me he needed a bigger allowance!

"After buying half a dozen desktop computers for my company's financial planners, I got the surprise of my life. Most of the executives were scared to death of them. I was having a terrible time trying to teach them to operate the program."

WHAT BLOOPER PHOBIA DOES TO ADULTS

After a week of frustration, Howard suddenly figured out what the problem was with his executives. They had Blooper Phobia. In fact, most adults do.

"I was thinking about how easily my son had learned to use the computer, and how difficult it seemed to be for the grown men and women. And then the reason struck me. Kids are not afraid to make mistakes. They haven't learned yet that mistakes are supposed to be bad. Grownups, especially the executive type, need to feel competent. They perceive making a mistake as a sign that a person is incompetent.

"But the fact is that learning something new requires making mistakes. Bloopers give you valuable feedback. It's like steering a car; when it starts to veer toward the center of the road (a mistake), you move the wheel slightly to the right. Eventually you learn how minor adjustments to the wheel keep the car on the straight and narrow.

"So how did I deal with the Blooper Phobia of my executives? I took them aside and told them they were expected to make mistakes with the computer; in fact, I wanted them too. I also encouraged them to take the machines home to practice there. Although I didn't say so, the reasoning behind this was that they would probably feel much less inhibited operating the keyboards in privacy. They could get all the trial and error they needed without fear of showing off their mistakes.

"The outcome? Within a week, each of the executives was happily using the financial planning program at his or her desk. I can't count the times they've wondered aloud how they ever got along without it."

DON'T LET BLOOPER PHOBIA HOLD YOU BACK

It's understandable that we adults don't like to make mistakes. We were brought up that way. Teachers in school rewarded us when we were right and punished us with poor grades when we were wrong. Our parents treated us the same way; so have many of our employers. But, as understandable as it may be, it's not right.

It's not right because, as Howard realized, any genuine learning experience involves trial and error. It's important not just in learning how to run equipment that is new to us, but in picking up any new skill.

If you make a certain pledge to yourself here and now—and keep that pledge whenever it applies in the future—I promise you will learn more and you'll learn faster. The pledge is to avoid fighting the mistakes you will inevitably make in picking up a new skill.

Accept the bloopers as part of the learning process. If you do this, you'll find that your bloopers become smaller and smaller. The beginner's errors will be succeeded by ones that can only be made at higher levels of knowledge. Again, it's like learning to steer a car. At first, you veer all over the road and overcorrect. But, after a while your jerking the wheel becomes less abrupt, until your oversteering and corrective steering are almost imperceptible.

SECRETS OF THE SUCCESSFUL

More than a dozen years ago, when I began writing and speaking publicly on the subject of personal success, I started to amass a wealth of research material that continues growing to this day. In the course of my work, I've encountered highly successful people in a broad variety of fields:

* Business
* Politics
* Entertainment
* Civic affairs
* Public service
* Religion
* Education

In consulting, working with, and writing about these people, I have discovered many individual elements of success—but few traits common to them all. Businessman A may have achieved his success because of his negotiating ability, while Politician B rose so high because of her engaging personality. There are, however, two similarities binding nearly all people who have achieved outstanding success. They share these two traits:

* A deep desire to succeed
* The knack of getting the most out of their brainpower

These people are thinkers, achievers, and succeeders not because they are so much brighter than the rest of the population; most of them are not. Because of their deep desire to succeed, they've learned how to make more efficient use of their most valuable asset—their minds.

Having decided to read this book, you've shown that you, too, have a deep desire to succeed. And now you are about to gain the second most common element of success—the ability to boost your brainpower.

So let's get started by improving your memory.

—2—

How to Get
Twice the Mileage
out of Your Memory

There are probably times when you think that you were
born with the world's worst memory. Facts you used to know
escape you now, when you need them. Figures and dates are
hard to recall. Names? Perhaps you have suffered through
awkward moments with people you've encountered unexpectedly—people who call you by name but whose own names
remain a blank in your mind.

And how about the times when you've fumbled for a particular word, only to have it elude you until half an hour later—
when you no longer need it?

Don't worry. Your memory is a lot better than you think.
It's just that you, like millions of other people, haven't learned
how to use it efficiently. Those facts, figures, names, and words
can become instantly available to you, ready to use whenever
you need them. All it takes is a slight adaptation in the way you
commit them to memory in the first place.

THE KEY TO A GOOD MEMORY

This chapter contains four distinct methods that will
greatly enhance the efficiency of your memory, allowing you to
recall much more information than has been possible until
now. The methods deal with:

1. General information
2. Numerical data
3. People's names
4. New words

Naturally, you want to strengthen your memory in these four vital categories. When you do, you'll be able to perform better in your dealings with other people, and you'll actually seem to be more intelligent. Right or wrong, people tend to rate the intelligence of others more on their memories than on their reasoning ability.

Each of the four methods is unique; it's geared to locking in a particular type of information. But all of them have one thing in common: their dependence on association. In one way or another, they have you remembering new information by associating it with something else that you know very well.

There are two requirements that must be met before any of the methods may be implemented:

1. Any fact that you want to remember must be thoroughly understood.
2. You must consciously decide you want to remember it.

How can you remember something you don't know? The answer is that you can't. That is one reason why you may have difficulty remembering the names of people you've met. You never really learned the names in the first place. Even when you do get a name correctly, you have no hope in the world of remembering it very long unless you determine that you will do so. Can you remember the last three telephone numbers you dialed? Of course not, because you had no desire to remember them when you dialed them.

Knowledge and desire alone, of course, are not enough. Once you determine that a certain fact, or set of facts, is to be remembered, you must have a method. That method must be both easy and infallible. The four methods outlined in this chapter meet these two criteria.

THE DATA INDEXING METHOD
FOR STORING AND RECALLING INFORMATION

First, let's get a big load off your shoulders. You don't need to remember nearly as much as you think you need to remember. In many cases, all you really need to remember is how and where to get information when it is required.

When Einstein was asked the number of feet in a mile, the great mathematician admitted he didn't know. He explained there was no reason to clutter his brain with information that could easily be looked up in a reference book.

When the *Chicago Tribune* printed an article calling Henry Ford stupid, he took the paper to court. It was up to the publisher to prove that the inventor was as stupid as the article had said he was. The publisher's lawyers asked him a series of questions on topics almost everyone is familiar with: names of Presidents, important dates in American history, etc.

Henry Ford was not able to answer many of the questions; and there was a good reason. He told the court that although he didn't know the answers, he could easily find someone to get the information for him.

Einstein and Ford had very little in common, but they did share one bit of knowledge that escapes most other people. They were familiar with the significance of this rule of Mental Leverage:

> It's far easier to remember where to get information when
> you need it than to memorize the information itself.

This is the basis of one of the simplest, and yet most powerful memory systems ever devised. Bank presidents use it, and so do salesmen and politicians. It's safe to say that unsuccessful people do NOT use it. It's known as the Data Indexing Method for storing and recalling information.

A television documentary recently featured a week in the life of a top American banking executive as he traveled from city to city, meeting with important officials and business leaders. It was clear that all of them respect him highly—and not just because of his position. Surprisingly, he explained his secret to the television audience.

Before leaving on such a trip, this executive has his staff put together loose-leaf folders giving him background on each of the people he is to meet. Then, while aboard the plane, he reviews the folder containing information on the people he is to meet in the next city. If you think the people he meets are highly impressed that he remembers so much about them, you're right. If you think his bank gets a lot more business from them than might otherwise be expected, you're right again.

HOW A LEADING SALESMAN REMEMBERS HIS CLIENTS

Ron R. is the top salesman in the insurance company where he works. No one else is able to come close to his volume of sales. Other salesmen who have occasionally traveled with him attribute his success to his "fabulous memory" concerning his clients.

As one of his colleagues told me: "Ron's memory for people, and facts about their families and personal interests, is no less than amazing. He may call on more than a dozen clients a day, and with each one he'll inquire about their families—identifying relatives by name—and talk about family interests, hobbies, and business achievements of the client. No wonder his clients like him so much."

When I met Ron and inquired about his memory system, he explained it this way:

"At the end of each day, I spend about twenty minutes making entries on small file cards—one for each person I've met that day. I jot down pertinent information about the person that I can bring up the next time we meet. Then, the next morning, just before starting out on my rounds, I pull out the file cards for the people I plan to meet that day. Referring to the appropriate card just before each meeting, I have all the information I need to let the person know I'm interested in him and care enough about him to remember things he's told me in the past. There's nothing better for making sales."

HOW YOU CAN USE THE DATA INDEXING METHOD

Please don't get the idea that you must, like the bank president, assemble loose-leaf folders, or, like Ron, keep a card file of pertinent information you wish to remember. I've related their experiences merely to demonstrate that Einstein was right. There is no need to clutter your brain with information that you will need only occasionally.

Entire books have been written to explain tricks for memorizing data that doesn't need to be memorized at all. It's far better to utilize your memory as an indexing system, telling you where to find information you need. This will give you access to a great deal more data than would otherwise be possible.

You might look at it this way: In a typical textbook, the index takes up about three percent of the total number of pages. Thus, each page of index gives you access to thirty-three pages of information. Using even the most powerful memory methods known to man, which would be easier to do—memorize one index page or thirty-three pages of text? The answer, of course, is the index, and that's why today's top performers in business, education, and science swear by the Data Indexing Method. It allows them to leverage their memory—multiplying their recall power by thirty-three or even more.

HOW TO MEET YOUR OWN MEMORY NEEDS

Unlike Ron R., most people don't keep card files on the people they want to remember. Chances are you're not a salesman calling on dozens of clients each week and you don't need to file information aimed at impressing them.

What you probably do need, if you're like most people, is a way to increase your ability to recall important information that you pick up in your daily reading. The method I'm about to describe is used by many of the world's most notable achievers—people who receive a steady stream of reports, memos, professional publications, books, and announcements. Do they memorize what they read? Of course not. But when they come across information that's important to them, they do commit to memory the location of that information.

As may be true in your case, these people frequently need to recall information at a moment's notice. The information may be one, two or more years old, and it must be instantly available to them. Thanks to the leverage provided by the Data Indexing Method, these people can greatly stretch their memory capacities.

Please realize that this method is not designed for learning entirely new subjects. Chapter 6 reveals speed-learning techniques that will have you picking up entirely new fields of knowledge and gaining a thorough comprehension in a surprisingly short period of time.

What we're talking about here, with the Data Indexing Method, is a means of locating isolated facts that may be needed for future reference. The facts may relate to your business, a hobby, or any pursuit that interests you.

Here's how some people I know use the Data Indexing Method:

* A physician uses it to keep track of the important information contained in the realms of medical literature he receives each week.

* A stockbroker who reads dozens of business publications uses it to remember where he read items of particular interest concerning companies he specializes in.

* A housewife who saves magazines that contain interesting recipes uses it to steer her to the right magazine when she's ready to try one of the specialties.

* An executive who must deal with a maze of constantly changing governmental regulations uses it to pinpoint rules that apply to whatever current work his office is doing.

Can the human brain really serve as an index to a great volume of material? The answer is yes, but not the kind of index that starts with A and ends with Z. In using the Data Indexing Method, you don't flash the alphabet through your mind until the right letter, and then the right word, pops up. The mind doesn't work that way.

Here's one way the mind does work:

You can permanently remember new information if you give it an interesting or unusual association.

In elementary school, I could never remember whether the man who headed the administration was the principal or the principle. Then one day, a teacher explained a way to differentiate the two words. "The principal of a school," she said, "is supposed to be your 'pal' and that's how his title is spelled." I'll never forget that spelling.

Perhaps in school you learned the names of the Great Lakes by using the word "HOMES"—standing for Huron, Ontario, Michigan, Erie, and Superior.

When you began music lessons, you learned the lines on the musical staff with the phrase "Every Good Boy Deserves Fun."

In each of these examples, the information to be remembered was given an interesting or unusual association: pal for principal, HOMES for the Great Lakes, and a phrase containing words starting with the lines comprising the treble clef staff. In each case, it's the interesting association that makes the information so easy to remember.

And these three examples provide you with a significant clue as to how you can create a constantly expanding mental index to all the written information you possess. You do it as the Mental Leverage experts do it—by associating the information with its source in an interesting or unusual way. Then, whenever you think of the information and want to refer to its source, you'll be instantly reminded of where to look.

Let's say, for example, that you have just read the chapter on making big money in mail order in my book, *Automatic Wealth-Building Formulas That Pile Up Riches Fast*. There's some valuable information in that chapter that you'll want to refer to later. But you have so many books, you may forget which one contained the mail order advice.

Here's how to apply the Data Indexing Method in such a case:

1. Give the information you wish to be indexed a label that identifies its subject. (In this case your Subject Label would be MAIL ORDER.)

2. Pick out a key word that identifies the source of the information. (In this case, the Source Identifier could be FORMULAS, one of the words in the title of the book.)

3. In an interesting or unusual way, create an association between the Subject Label and the Source Identifier. (In this case, work out an association between MAIL ORDER and FORMULAS.)

In the above case, you might picture yourself operating a mail order business that deals in some sort of formulas. Most people find that the more ludicrous the association, the easier it is to remember. Thus, you could picture the mail order business as one that sells baby formulas. Make that picture vivid in your mind. Spend a moment or two picturing yourself taking orders for and mailing out baby formulas. You might even picture babies devouring the formulas that you sell.

If you do this, the next time you think of mail order and want to recall which book contained the fascinating chapter on that subject, you'll think immediately of the book with *Formulas* in the title.

A POWERFUL MEMORY SYSTEM

You can see that the association—your running a mail order business featuring baby formulas—is so interesting and unusual that you'll remember it for as long as your interest in mail order continues. In addition to being interesting and unusual, it's meaningful to you. And that's what will bring it back to mind whenever you need it.

"What happens," you wonder, "if I have several information sources all on the same topic?"

Simple as it is, this is indeed a powerful memory system, and it allows for as many information sources as you want. Let's say you would like to place in your mental index another of my books that also contains information on mail order. The book is entitled *Spare-Time Businesses You Can Start and Run for Less than $1,500.*

Let's use the $1,500 as our Source Identifier, since you probably don't own any other books with that in the title. All you need do is expand the mental picture of your mail order business so that it has you selling formulas for $1,500 each. Ridiculous? Of course. And that's why it works.

If you have many different information sources on the same topic, and you want to remember them all, then you'll do just as the creator of a written index does. You'll have various subheadings under the main topic. You may, for example, have a number of listings dealing with mail order—too many to lump together. What you do in that case is put the sources in various categories. You might have "mail order advertising" as one Subject Label and "catalogs" as another. Then you can combine one or more Source Identifiers with each of these Subject Labels and create mental images that will bring them instantly to mind.

One of the great advantages of this system is that you are never consciously memorizing anything. You don't have to.

My physician friend who uses it to keep track of new medical information says, "I find it fun to dream up those weird associations. After bringing a new one to mind, I lean back, close my eyes for a second or two, and then mentally picture it. That permanently implants it in my memory, and when I need to refer to that particular bit of medical information again, I know precisely where to look."

USE DIGIT CONVERSIONS TO REMEMBER FIGURES AND DATES

You may have seen—or at least read about—demonstrations in which "mental wizards" reel off a long series of numbers with total accuracy. You may know other people who have the phone numbers of hundreds of their friends and business associates down pat. Perhaps you work with somebody who knows the numbers of his own, and his wife's, Social Security accounts, charge cards, checking accounts, car license plates, and driver's licenses.

It's safe to say that all of these people use the same method. They convert the digits they want to remember to words, and then remember the words. Numbers are difficult to remember—especially when there are a lot of them. You can't picture digits the way you can words. For example, which of the following do you think you could remember easier:

32155846   Mental Leverage

Of course, it's much easier to remember the phrase. You may be surprised to learn that people who use digit conversions would instantly know that Mental Leverage stands for 32155846. And they might use that two-word phrase to remember that eight-digit number.

How do they do it? Even if you have no current need to

memorize a lot of numbers, you'll want an overview of how it's done. At first glance, the method may seem complicated, but it's not.

As you know, there are ten digits in the decimal system. In this method of remembering numbers, each of those ten digits is assigned a consonant sound, or a group of similar sounds. For example, the digit 1 corresponds with the sound created by a t or a d. Agreed, t and d don't make identical sounds, but they're close enough for our purposes.

Why do you want to convert numbers to consonants? Simply so that you can take those consonant sounds and make a word or phrase out of them—a word or phrase that is easily remembered. And just as the numbers can be converted to that word or phrase, the word or phrase can later be converted back to the number.

For example, consider the consonants contained in the phrase Mental Leverage. Here they are, with the corresponding numbers listed below them:

M N T L L V R G

3 2 1 5 5 8 4 6

Remember we said that t or d can be substituted for 1? You see it done above.

All you have to know to make this system work are the ten consonant sounds that correspond with the ten digits. If, for instance, you wanted to memorize 32155846, you'd know that the corresponding consonants are MNTLLVRG. That group of letters in itself is meaningless, but it can be formed into the phrase Mental Leverage. It could also be the following:

> Mental love rage
> My nightly ale average

Let's take a closer look at the second of the two listings.

The first word has just one consonant sound: M

The second word has three consonant sounds: N, T, and L

The third word has one consonant sound: L

The fourth word has three consonant sounds: V, R, and G

Thus we have MNTLLVRG. And to those who know how to convert consonants to digits, we also have 32155846.

Now let's learn how to do just that—convert between digits and consonants and back again. The chart below lists (1) the digits, (2) the corresponding sounds, and (3) a memory peg to help you associate 1 and 2. Note that because there are more than ten consonants in the alphabet, similar sounds are lumped together, leaving us with just ten.

Some of the memory pegs will seem farfetched or silly but please remember something you learned earlier: the more ludicrous an association, the easier it is to remember.

Digit	Corresponding Sound	Memory Peg
1	t or d	There is 1 downstroke in a small t
2	n	There are 2 downstrokes in a small n
3	m	There are 3 downstrokes in a small m
4	r	The digit 4 (four) ends in r
5	l	Your 5 fingers, with thumb out, form an L
6	j, ch, sh, soft g	There are 6 letters in SHucks
7	k, hard c, hard g	By moving two 7's around, you get a K
8	f, ph, v	A handwritten f looks like an 8
9	p or b	Hold a 9 up to a mirror and you see a p
0	soft c, s, z	The final digit is 0, and the final letter in the alphabet is z

Reading the chart over several times, and then referring to it as needed, will enable you to learn the associations in very short order. Whenever you have a free moment, think of a digit and try to arrive quickly at its corresponding sound. Before long, you'll find that you no longer need the memory pegs; the numbers and the sounds have become "joined" in your mind. You'll know without thinking about it that 1 means t or d, and 8 means the f or v sound.

The next, and final, step in learning the digit conversion system is to practice converting numbers to phrases and back again. It's the first part that takes the longest. You saw, for example, that the letters MNTLLVRG could form several phrases; but any phrase made up of those eight letters can only convert to 32155846. Thus, if you chose Mental Leverage, mental love rage, or my nightly ale average, you would still have the same consonants—and each of those consonants can only stand for one digit.

Let's take another number at random: 3845912. This gives us the following consonant sounds:

MFRLPTN

This could form the phrase "my for-real put-on" which doesn't make much sense except that for-real and put-on are opposites and thus the phrase is just crazy enough to be remembered.

Now, to prove the system works, take this phrase and look up each of the consonant sounds in the chart. What number do you come up with?

Digit conversions are used most often by people who want to remember a long series of phone numbers or, in some cases, serial numbers of products they work with. You might, for instance, have 100 or more phone numbers that you must call from time time, and you'd like to be spared the effort of looking each one up every time you need it. Wouldn't it be great to be able to remember 100 phone numbers? We'll take one number and, step-by-step, see how it's implanted firmly in your memory. Let's assume you want to remember the number of your attorney.

1. Convert the digits to consonants. Let's say that 786-4372 is your lawyer's phone number. The consonant sounds are KFJRMKN.

2. Use the consonant sounds to form one or more words associated with your lawyer. Remember, it's the sounds, not the specific letters, that count. In the above example, the first sound, k, could also be a hard c or hard g. The sounds in KFJRMKN could form these three words: CouGH, GeRM, CaN (the consonant sounds are capitalized). In the first word, GH is pronounced like an F.

3. Because ridiculous associations are more easily remembered, you could associate the three words with your lawyer this way: He defends a COUGH for spreading a GERM, but loses and the germ is thrown in the CAN. COUGH leads to GERM, which leads to CAN. Actually picture your lawyer defending a cough that had spread a germ and was sentenced to the can. When you dream up such an image yourself, it stays with you permanently.

If all this sounds farfetched to you, it is. And that's why it works for those who sincerely try it. People who use the method point out these facts:

* After some practice, converting numbers to consonants and back again becomes almost automatic. The mind thinks of 362 as MJN.

* Converting consonants to words also becomes much easier with practice. It would take an experienced "converter" only a second or two to convert MJN into MOTION. (Remember that J can also be an SH sound.)

* Converting back to digits is the easiest of all. Once you have a word or phrase, you merely take the consonant sounds and substitute the corresponding digits. The sounds in MOTION are: M and SH and N, and that equals 362. (In the case of short numbers, some people use the consonants as the first letter of each word in a phrase. MJN=My Jiving Niece.)

* When you have a lot of numbers to remember, the time it takes to convert them to word images will be amply repaid by never having to look them up again.

Although you may not presently have the need to memorize great lists of numbers, you now know that it can be done. When the time comes that you do need this kind of memory ability, you know where to look to find the best method—the one that has been used by memory experts worldwide for centuries. By learning the consonant equivalents of the ten digits and practicing number-word conversions, you'll enjoy the same numerical memory skills that have been practiced by the top experts.

ENJOY TOTAL NAME RECALL WITH THE LINKAGE TECHNIQUE

If you have trouble remembering other people's names, you're hurting yourself a lot more than you may realize. People love to hear their names used. An easy way to hold someone else's attention is to use his or her name frequently. On the other hand, the easiest way to lose a person's interest and confidence is to forget his or her name.

Forgetting a person's name—one of his most important possessions—is among the worst insults you can make. It shows you don't care, and this can rob you of:

* Friendships
* Business relationships
* Respect
* Employment opportunities
* Career advancements

Why then do so many people forget names? It's because they haven't learned this fact:

> Mental Leverage makes it far easier to remember names than it is to fumble your way out of the awkward situation that occurs when you forget someone's name ... or, worse, use the wrong name.

Have you ever been in that sort of situation? Perhaps you've run into someone unexpectedly—someone whose name is on the tip of your tongue—and you are embarrassed by not actually remembering it. This need never happen again, once you apply the five-step system you are about to learn.

* STEP ONE: Make a conscious decision that from now on you will learn and remember the name of every person to whom you are introduced. Remind yourself of this decision daily, and each time you are about to be introduced to someone.

* STEP TWO: As the introduction takes place, make sure you get the person's name right. If necessary, ask for it to be repeated and perhaps even spelled out.

* STEP THREE: As you acknowledge the introduction, repeat the name, and continue using it throughout the conversation.

* STEP FOUR: Associate the name with a physical characteristic, a personality trait, or some other peculiarity that will remind you of that person. This is known as the Linkage Technique. Farfetched links are not only permitted, they are encouraged. Perhaps you've just

met Mr. Everett, who is very thin. Picture him as a hill-billy who says, "I ain't ever et." Of course, it's silly, but you'll never forget who he is.

*STEP FIVE: At the end of the day, make a written note of each person you have met just to firm it up in your mind. From time to time, go over these written records of newly acquired names. Use the Linkage Technique to obtain a mental picture of the person and his or her name.

Which of these five steps is the most important? The many name experts who use this program will attest that they are equally important. Omit one of them, and you have weakened your ability to remember names. Use them all, and your success is assured. Let's see why each of them is so important:

* Making a conscious decision to learn and remember names—and frequently reminding yourself of that de-cision—gets you over one of the biggest bugaboos to name recalling: getting the name in the first place. We concentrate so much on what we are going to say that the name of the person we are meeting flies right past us. Being absolutely determined to learn the name gets us over this problem and thus is the vital first step.

* Getting a person's name wrong is perhaps the only thing worse than not getting it at all. The process of being sure you have it right has a second benefit: it serves to strengthen your memory of the name.

* Any school child can tell you that repetition is a strong memory aid. Repeating the name while you are talking with, and looking directly at, a person builds a lasting mental association.

* The Linkage Technique is surprisingly effective, using the same memory principle you've seen in action earlier in this chapter: outlandish mental images that bring the desired fact, number, or name instantly to mind. And if you think about it, you'll realize that a lasting memory image can be made of any name. Travalini? Picture someone who always "travels lean." Rosenburg? She grows roses on an iceberg.

* Taking a moment at the end of the day to write down
  the names of those you've met serves two purposes: it
  tests and strengthens the memory images you've formed,
  and it allows you to review them periodically.

HOW TO BUILD A WORD BANK
OF DYNAMIC TERMS AND EXPRESSIONS

One of the ways other people judge you is by the words
you use, and how you use them. Thus your vocabulary, and
more particularly your verbal skills (as educators like to call
them), have a lot to do with your success in life.

There are several things you should know right off:

* You don't need a huge vocabulary to impress other
  people.
* Even if your current vocabulary is limited, adding 100–
  200 words is probably all you need.
* By picking the right words to learn, those 100 or 200
  words will do the work of 1000 or more.

This is another example of how Mental Leverage pays off.
Business consultants agree: there is no need to take expensive
and time-consuming vocabulary-improvement courses. There
is no need to memorize long lists of big new words. There is, in
fact, no need to use big words at all—unless they are professional terms commonly used in your line of work.

All you need is this natural way to expand your vocabulary, giving it the dynamic terms and expressions that will
convince other people that you are an intelligent and learned
person—without appearing to be a showoff.

It's the method used by Alan V.—a young man who had
never completed high school—to win a promotion normally
granted only to college graduates. Alan was employed as a field
service technician for an office supply firm.

"Field service technician," Alan explains, "is a fancy title
for repairman. I repaired typewriters and copy machines for a
major manufacturer, doing the work in the 'field'—meaning
customers' offices.

"I was fairly happy in the job until one day I figured something out. The company was charging its customers fifty dollars an hour for my services, but it was paying me less than ten dollars. Sure, the company was entitled to a reasonable profit on my labor, but where was the rest of the money going? It suddenly dawned on me that my sweat—and that of the other technicians—was paying the juicy salaries of the service executives who never went out in the field at all.

"From the cars they drove and the homes they lived in, I knew these executives were earning a lot more than ten dollars an hour. I also knew that if I wanted to climb up into their ranks, I'd have to let them know I was too smart to be an hourly worker. The only way to make such an impression, I realized, was the way I spoke and wrote; the words I used and the way I put them together."

Alan knew that a crash vocabulary course was not the answer. Material learned through rote memorizing is quickly forgotten. Instead, he opted for a method he read of in one of my magazine articles. He quickly realized that, as the article stated, it is one of the simplest, most effective word-building methods ever devised.

Here's all that is required:

1. Keep a small notebook in your pocket at all times, so that whenever you see or hear a word you don't fully understand, you can write it down.

2. Later, when it's practical to do so, look up the most recent words you have acquired. After determining what they mean, try to recall the way they were used when you read or heard them. Think of them in that context, and in possible other uses. Decide which words you want to "keep."

3. Start using these words in your own conversation. Get to feel comfortable with them. This will firm them up in your memory.

4. From time to time, go over the older entries in your word notebook. Renew your acquaintance with any important words that have slipped from your current usage.

"I found right away that the method worked," Alan says. "I was picking up a dozen or more powerful new words each week, and using them in my conversation. And there's something else I discovered: not only was my vocabulary improving, but so was my sentence structure. Paying attention to what people said and how they said it made me much more conscious of my own word usage.

"This was obviously noticed by some people who count, because when a management position opened up, I was chosen. It was the first time in six years they had picked someone from the technician ranks. The usual practice had been to hire college graduates. In my case, I had probably begun to sound so much like a college graduate myself that I seemed a natural for the management opening."

Whether or not you are looking for a promotion, and regardless of your current vocabulary level, you can give yourself a big boost by following the same word-building program that paid off handsomely for Alan. It takes so little time that it's almost effortless, and yet it will return a lifetime of dividends. Not the least of these dividends will be the ability to gain a better understanding of everything you read.

And that brings us to the subject of High-Performance Reading, a skill you'll acquire in the next chapter.

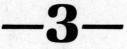

—3—

The Key to
High-Performance
Reading

The key to High-Performance Reading is, in one word, leverage. The same amount of time and effort that you now devote can have you getting at least twice as much reading done—and with better recall of what you've read. People who practice High-Performance Reading (HPR) find their reading a lot more enjoyable, too.

Sure, their eyes are zipping across pages in the time to takes some people to read a paragraph, but they're getting as much knowledge and enjoyment out of it as slowpokes do, and probably even more. As you pick up HPR skills, you'll enjoy the same benefits.

HOW TO READ MORE AND GET MORE
FROM WHAT YOU READ

You've probably heard about speed readers who achieve a pace of 1200 or even 1800 words per minute. Perhaps you've read an article on how to speed read and have tried doing it yourself.

Most people—even those with a seemingly natural flair for speed reading—don't like it. They don't enjoy working frantically to keep up a superhuman pace, and they often find that they have to go back over what they've read to bone up on points they missed.

This should be good news for you:

> High-Performance Reading makes it possible to read and absorb as much important material as a speed reader does—without racing at the speed reader's pace.

In other words, you don't have to be a speed reader in order to enjoy speed-reading benefits. Here's why:

* Doubling your reading speed, instead of multiplying it five or six times, is much easier and more enjoyable. When this double speed is combined with special efficiency techniques, your total reading performance is greatly enhanced.

* About half your current reading effort is wasted. Learning how to eliminate the waste allows you to devote the same time to reading that counts—thereby doubling your input.

* By employing the Visual Outline Technique, you can rapidly find the key phrases and paragraphs in any document—skimming over the introductory and extraneous material that adds nothing to your knowledge.

Thus, High-Performance Reading increases your reading efficiency in a number of ways:

1. It reveals how to heighten your reading speed by as much as 100 percent with very little effort—and allows you to forget the agonies of trying to keep up a 1500-wpm race.

2. It apportions your reading time so that you can digest as much informative material as a 1500-wpm speed reader.

3. It steers you directly to the "meat" of any piece of writing, showing how you can instantly recognize the many lines of "fat" that don't have to be read.

An accomplished speed reader can go through a typical book in about two hours. If in a given week he spends ten hours reading books, he'll probably complete five volumes. But he'll have worked very hard doing that. On the other hand, in the same amount of time, the person who uses HPR will glean just as much from his reading—perhaps even more—and have a lot more fun doing it.

Typical of those who use HPR is Veronica D., who gulped down twenty diet books in less than a week.

"When I decided the time had come to go on a diet," Veronica explained, "I wanted to be sure that the diet I picked was one I could stick with over a period of many months. Of course, there are always diet books on the best-seller list—but who knows if today's fad diet is any better than whatever was popular five, ten, or even fifteen years ago?"

Veronica decided that the best way to find out was to go to the library and check out every diet book on its shelves—a total of twenty. She was able to go through all twenty books in less time than speed readers would take, yet she learned as much about the diets explained in the books as anyone could, reading at any speed.

Veronica learned HPR many years ago and has made a career of teaching it to corporate executives who face a heavy load of reading to keep up with their work. Corporations of all sizes hire her to conduct in-house seminars for their executives. The proof of her success—and that of HPR—is that these same companies invite her back year after year to teach more executives.

The HPR techniques outlined in this chapter are the same as those taught by Veronica. They'll work for you as well as they work for her—and the thousands of clients who have multiplied their reading efficiency as a result of her courses.

THE SECRET OF CONCATENATION

When you link two things together, you concatenate them. The word "to" is a concatenation of the letters "t" and "o." When you see "to" inscribed on paper, you don't think of the two letters it contains; you think of the word as one entity. It's the same with longer words. Once you become familiar with them, you see them as one word rather than a grouping of letters.

To a certain extent you even do this with words that are new to you. For example, the first time you saw the word "concatenation" you didn't examine each of the thirteen letters individually. Instead, you examined the syllables: con-cat-e-na-tion. Each of the syllables is, of course, a concatenation of letters.

The trouble with most readers is that while they are able to concatenate letters and syllables, they don't carry it to the next logical step: they don't concatenate words. We are taught in school to learn individual words, and for the rest of our lives we read individual words.

HPR, on the other hand, has you reading thoughts and phrases instead of individual words. Here's a simple example:

Read faster.

It's composed of two words. Unless you've taken Veronica's course or heard me speak on HPR, you probably read that phrase by examining its two words: READ and FASTER. With a little bit of practice, however, you could just as easily have seen it as one unit instead of two.

You're in for a pleasant surprise when you learn how much faster you can read merely by concatenating words—by reading phrases and thoughts instead of individual words. It's a knack you can pick up rapidly, and you can start your practice right now, as you read this chapter.

For most of our lives each of us has been guilty of pausing slightly after each word we read. We give our brains a split second to let the meaning of each word sink in. Why not schedule that pause after each phrase instead of each word?

Let's take the last sentence of the preceding paragraph. Instead of reading:

Why
not
schedule
that
pause
after
each
phrase
instead
of
each
word?

read it this way:

> Why not schedule
> that pause
> after each phrase
> instead of
> each word?

Your pause after each word may be so brief that it's imperceptible. Although you're probably not aware of it, proof that it exists can be seen in the increased reading speed that you develop when you actually begin reading phrases instead of words.

As you read, concentrate on picking out written thoughts; they may consist of two, three, or even as many as five or six words. The more words you can read at one glance, the faster your overall reading speed will become

People sometimes question me about the phrase "at one glance." Their presumption is that all reading is done at one glance. True, you may read several paragraphs or even several pages before you lift your eyes from the paper, but in the course of doing all that reading you have made dozens and perhaps hundreds of glances. That's how many times your eyes halt, however briefly, on a word or phrase. Each time your eyes stop to pick up new information, it is considered a glance."

Your first goal, in developing the skills of HPR, is to make those glances occur as far apart as possible. Naturally, as you start out, each glance will provide an input of as few as two words. But as you pick up practice, you'll be able to enlarge the scope of your glances, and the speed of your reading will rise accordingly.

Remember, your goal is NOT to become a speed reader. You don't have to develop a pace of 1500 or even 1000 wpm. The efficiency techniques you learn later will make up the difference between those ultra-high speeds and what your actual rate is.

AGATHA CHRISTIE, MAYBE . . . OTHERS, NO

Mystery writer Agatha Christie liked to fill her novels with clues—some important, others put there to trick you. Read all the clues, pick the right ones, put them together, and you might come to the same conclusion as the author as to who the murderer was. But, more often than not, you wouldn't guess correctly.

Fortunately for the person who has a great deal of serious reading to do, most writers don't bury clues in their texts. The reports, memos, trade publications, and correspondence that you receive were written to inform, not confuse you. You don't have to study every word looking for ulterior motives and devious distractions.

The people who write most of the material you read may not be nearly as talented as Agatha Christie was, but they do succeed in making their points much clearer. Perhaps it pays to linger over words and passages in a Christie novel, but it's downright costly to do so in nearly every other type of writing.

Your plan, then, is look for thoughts and ideas instead of words. What is the writer driving at? What is the information he wants you to obtain—and what information is important to you? This is on your mind as you progress through a piece of reading. As you keep pushing ahead, you may miss words or groups of words, but you pick up enough to get the overall meaning. And when you're through, you've gotten the full message the author wanted to convey, even though you may not remember the precise words he used.

Efficient readers are active readers, not passive ones. They're not content in having the words (or even phrases) flow past them as if on a conveyor belt. Instead, they seek out the important, descriptive, and meaningful ideas. As they read, they're actively searching. The object of their search, of course, is information that is valuable to them, or, in the case of reading for entertainment, interesting to them.

The average adult reads at a rate of less than 250 wpm. Using concatenation, and becoming an active reader, will easily allow you to double that speed. And you can accomplish it in a week or two. Just practice with all of the reading you do.

Merely doubling your reading speed (and you'll be effectively doing a lot better than that before I'm through with you) can pack a tremendous wallop where you work. Most people in clerical and executive positions spend at least ⅓ of their day reading. That's 2.6 hours. When you double your reading speed, you can either:

(a) do twice as much reading as before, or

(b) do the same amount of reading in half the time.

In either case, your value has shot up by 16.6 percent, which is the amount of time you have saved for additional reading or other duties. Thus,

IF YOUR WEEKLY PAY HAS BEEN:	YOU ARE NOW WORTH:
$ 200	$ 233
300	350
400	466
500	583
600	700
700	816
800	933
900	1049
1000	1166

If anything, these figures are conservative. Veronica D., who has taught thousands of people how to use HPR in tripling or quadrupling their reading speeds, says she's seen her "graduates" move rapidly up the job ladder—much more rapidly than could otherwise be expected. Naturally, their pay was increased along with their responsibilities, and usually at a considerably higher percentage rate than is indicated by the above table.

In my own dealings with corporate executives, I've learned the same thing. Executives whose job it is to rate people under them tell me that high-performance readers just naturally become high-performance workers, and their skills are recognizd and rewarded accordingly.

Naturally, the same skills that make you adept at HPR on the job will benefit you in your personal reading. Veronica's twenty diet books provide a perfect example. By the time somebody else might have completed the third book, Veronica had gobbled them all and was starting on the diet of her choice.

Perhaps diet books are not your bag—but news magazines and history books are. The same techniques that advance you in your career will multiply the amount of important personal reading you achieve.

THE BONUS SPEEDER-UPPER

Before we move on to the efficiency techniques that will make you a truly high-performance reader, here's a tip on how to speed up your reading without any effort. Less effort, in fact, than you are now putting in.

Read raster with less effort? Absolutely. At first, you may not appreciate the full value of the advice you're about to receive, but start using it in your daily reading and you'll find that your speed is indeed enhanced. Here's the tip:

If you've missed a word or point, don't linger and don't go back.

It's as simple as that. Whether you realize it or not, a significant percentage of your reading time is spent going back over material you have just read. Perhaps you want to double-check what was said, or you missed the point, or a later sentence jumped out at you, catching your attention and causing you to bypass what remained of the sentence you had been reading.

Reading experts note that ninety-nine times out of a hundred you gain nothing by going back over the material. Instead, it's greatly to your advantage to move ahead. By the time you are through reading the article, report, letter (or whatever), the point you missed will undoubtedly be covered again, if it was at all important. Only if, after completing the article, the point you missed still needs refreshing, then you should go back over it. And that will be rare.

Expect a surprise when you start trying to stop rereading material. It's going to be more difficult than you think. You've built up a habit over the years, and habits are hard to break even when breaking them means less effort. Fortunately, there's a prop you can use to help you. A small slip of paper or a file card will do the trick. If you have trouble ridding yourself of the nasty rereading habit, cover up lines immediately after reading them. Don't let your eyes be tempted.

Breaking the rereading habit can improve your reading speed by more than twenty percent.

EMPLOY THE VISUAL OUTLINE TECHNIQUE

We've spoken several times in this chapter about reading rates of 1500 wpm, and how such high-velocity pacing should NOT be your goal. There are a number of reasons:

* It isn't words-per-minute that count, it's ideas per minute. Because you are no longer looking at individual words, counting them has no meaning. You are reading for information, not words.

* Concentrating on word speed forces you to read many more words than are necessary. You can absorb all of the ideas an author wanted to convey without reading all of the words he wrote.

* Speed readers are not usually good comprehenders. They read rapidly, but if they claim to recall and understand all they have read, they're fooling themselves. On the other hand, the person who reads for ideas knows what he's looking for, what he sees, and what he's learned.

Thus, when high-performance readers measure their reading speed, it's listed as an EQUIVALENT of so many words per minute. When you read at an equivalent of 2000 wpm, you are absorbing 2000 words worth of printed information per minute. Your eyes have not actually locked in on 2000 words each minute, but your mind has received all of the important information that the author chose to convey in that many words.

When I relayed the above information to a group of government agency heads recently, one of them asked me: "Don't you really mean that such a person is skimming?"

I prefer to call it the Visual Outline Technique, because it's more than skimming. A person who employs this technique has one quality that's particularly notable. He or she is IMPATIENT. This reader wants the author to get to the point immediately, and if the author fails to do it, then the reader does it for him by zooming ahead until pertinent information is found.

But if the person who uses the Visual Outline Technique is impatient, he is also very well organized. And those two qualities—impatience and organization—are the keys to his success.

The difference between skimming and Visual Outlining is like the difference between reading a newspaper and reading an encyclopedia.

* You "read" a newspaper by scanning the headlines and choosing whatever stories catch your interest.

* You "read" an encyclopedia by locating the specific information you want and then going directly to the section(s) containing that information.

"But," you argue, "the average book I pick up doesn't have all of its information as neatly categorized as an encyclopedia does, and besides, when I read a book, I'm looking for all the author can tell me, not just for individual bits of information."

That's a mistake. Why take everything the author has to tell you? He has probably used two or three times as many words as were necessary. You can learn just as much—in considerably less time—by taking these steps:

1. Before you begin examining a book, article, or other piece of writing, know why you want to read it. What specific knowledge are you seeking?

2. Learn how the piece of writing is organized. Examine the table of contents and index, if any, and then rapidly preview the pages, glancing at sections here and there to give yourself a good idea of what the work contains and how it's laid out.

3. Determine which parts, if any, can be skipped without causing you to miss the information you are seeking. (If you don't like to pay twelve or fifteen dollars for a book and then skip some of its contents, console yourself with the fact that printed matter is permanent and can always be referred to later, when leisure time allows.)

4. If you are not looking for specific information, but want the gist of the entire work, concentrate on the preface and introductory material, chapter titles, section sub-heads, and summaries. Go rapidly over the body of text until you encounter material that's important to you.

5. When you do encounter text that is important to you, read by paragraph instead of by word or sentence. Picking up this knack is easy, as you're about to learn.

HOW TO READ BY PARAGRAPH

Your preview of the written work (examining the introductory material, index, section and chapter titles, etc.) has given you a good idea of the type of information it contains, and how that information is presented. Now it's time to dig in—to get the "meat" contained in all that verbiage.

The most efficient way to do it is to consider the text as a series of paragraphs. Think of each paragraph as a self-contained unit with its own message to convey. Grasp that message as rapidly as possible, and after you've got it, move swiftly to the next paragraph. Don't linger over supplemental material that merely serves to expand on the message you've already grasped in a particular paragraph.

As you become skilled at reading by paragraph, here's what you'll find:

* It will become increasingly easy to grasp the message of most paragraphs right away.

* You'll know almost at once whether the paragraph contains vital information that deserves closer scrutiny, or whether to go on to the next paragraph.

* Being able to glide over some paragraphs, devoting extra attention only to the important ones, will get you through the entire piece of writing with much greater speed than would otherwise be possible.

* The technique of reading by paragraph is particularly helpful when you are searching for specific information in an article or book, but don't know where to find it. Instead of skimming, as most people do, use your ability to grasp paragraph messages rapidly, moving quickly from paragraph to paragraph until the required information is found.

Fortunately for the beginning paragraph reader, the message in most paragraphs is delivered fairly early. You don't have to search many lines before you know what the writer wants to convey. And after the point is made, it's usually followed by sentences that merely illustrate or expand on that point.

Let's take, as an example, a paragraph from my most recent book. This is from *Control Dynamics for Mastery Over People* (Parker Publishing Company, Inc., West Nyack, N.Y.):

> Nearly everything you want out of life can be given to you by other people. If you think about it for a moment, you'll realize how much you depend on others for the good things you seek. Job promotions, success in business, close friendships, influence in your community: these are just a few of the advantages that you can gain only by dealing successfully with others.

As in many paragraphs, the point is made in the first sentence. That's the meat, and everything else is gravy. After reading the first sentence, you can move your eyes rapidly over the remaining lines just to be certain there is no extra message. In most cases, there won't be.

Of course, writers like variety. Sometimes they lead up to the message, putting the gravy first, and placing the message, or main point, at the end of the paragraph. Here again, practice will be of great assistance to you. You'll recognize these paragraphs right away, and you'll see signals telling you to move quickly through the "gravy" sections to where the "meat" is located.

The point to remember:

> Stick with a paragraph only as long as it takes you to grasp its message; then move promptly to the next paragraph.

The law of averages is very much in your favor. Most of the time you'll get the message before you are halfway through the paragraph. And this means another doubling of your reading speed.

REINFORCING WHAT YOU READ

The prospect of being able to zip through three, four, or more times as much reading material in a given period of time worries some people. They often say something like this to me:

"Sure, I can see how my comprehension of what I'm reading will be just as good, but how much will I actually remember later? With all that information flying past my eyes, a lot of it is bound to be forgotten."

It won't be forgotten if you reinforce it. As you know, the word reinforce means to strengthen or support, and there is an easy and yet effective way to strengthen and support your memory of what you've read. All it involves is a brief mental review, undertaken at some point after you have finished your reading.

In the course of everyone's day there are several periods in which there is no particular demand on the mind. These periods occur while you're driving a car, walking down the street, waiting in a doctor's office, eating a meal, showering, etc. Your mind is free to do as it will. Many of us daydream during some of these periods, but you can also use one or more of them to reinforce material you have recently read.

It's a simple procedure. Merely think back on what you learned in your last reading session. Review the important points and any related information relayed by the author. To make it easier, there are five questions you can ask yourself about what you've read. As you'll see, the questions deal with subjects whose first letters are contained in the word SMART. Use this word as a memory prodder.

Subject:	What was the piece about?
Material:	What important information was presented?
Assertions:	What, if any, opinions did the writer present?
Reaction:	What is your opinion of the piece?
Trademark:	Name one element of the piece that makes it stand apart.

This type of mental review works for the same reason that a discussion in a classroom reinforces what the students have read in their textbooks. The discussion may contain absolutely no information that they haven't read, but the human mind works in such a way that when they talk about what they've read, the information becomes firmly implanted in their memories.

True, when you conduct your brief mental review there is

no teacher on hand and there are no other people taking part in the "discussion." However, as far as your mind is concerned, the effect is the same. The simple process of recalling recent reading material and thinking about it makes it "yours"—something that will remain in your memory.

NO COST TO YOU

One of the great advantages of this mental reinforcement method is that it is done during periods when you:

(a) would normally be killing time, or

(b) are involved in a physical activity that makes few demands on your mind.

You use some of that time—and usually it need be only a minute or two—to lock up the knowledge you gained in your last reading session. It puts the finishing touch on HPR, guaranteeing that you'll gain a lasting benefit from what you've read.

In finding the time to do this, you probably won't have to go to the extremes that a friend of mine goes to, whose duty it is to attend a number of business conferences and seminars each week.

Here's what Ashley S. says:

Whenever one of the speakers gets particularly long-winded, others in the room naturally start daydreaming. But not I. Instead, I go over some of the recent High-Performance Reading that I've done. This makes even the dullest meeting worthwhile.

THE FIVE STEPS TO HIGH-PERFORMANCE READING

What you have seen in this chapter is a five-step program followed by today's most accomplished High-Performance Readers. They have proven that it is better than speed reading because it zips you through more material in less time, and with greater comprehension.

Take it one step at a time. Do not move on to the second step until you've become proficient in the one you've been working on. You'll probably be able to pick up the skills a lot quicker than you think.

Here, in capsule form, are the five steps.

1. Develop the knack of concatenation. Stop reading one word at a time and develop the habit of joining several words and reading them as one unit.

2. Become an active, rather than a passive, reader. Instead of reading individual words, actively search out the important, descriptive, and meaningful ideas. Move rapidly over other material.

3. Don't linger or go back. A surprising amount of most people's reading time is spent going back over material that has just been read. As difficult as it may be to break this nonproductive habit, doing so will pay tremendous speed dividends. A prop that can help you is a small slip of paper held over lines you have just read.

4. Read by paragraph. First, skim through the introductory material, section and chapter titles, index, and any other "signposts" to get a feel for what the piece contains. Then, treat the body of the text as a series of paragraphs, each paragraph being a self-contained unit with its own message to convey. As soon as you've grasped the message, move immediately on to the next paragraph and repeat the process.

5. Reinforce what you've read. At the earliest opportunity after doing some High-Performance Reading, use the S.M.A.R.T. self-questioning technique to remind yourself of what you've read, and to have it implanted permanently in your memory.

WHEN SLOW READING PAYS OFF

Even the most proficient High-Performance Readers take a break once in a while. As Veronica D. points out:

HPR is for business and information reading. For pure entertainment, for pure joy, there's nothing like leaning back in an armchair and reading a novel or a book of poetry or the work of an ancient philosopher as slowly as you can, savoring every word. Certainly, ninety percent of my own reading is done HPR style. But every so often, when I have some free time for relaxation, I purposely shift out of those high-speed reading gears and proceed in low-low. I find it totally refreshing.

So take it from Veronica. Even though you must break yourself of a lifetime of bad reading habits, you shouldn't forget them entirely. Bring them out of the closet every once in a while when you feel like rewarding yourself. But treat this reward as you would a high-calorie dessert—to be indulged in only occasionally so it doesn't undo all the good habits you've developed.

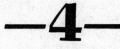

Quick Math
Without a Calculator

Calculators are wonderful things. They can do in seconds what used to take us minutes of manual figuring. They're so cheap that anyone can afford one. The equivalent of a calculator that once sold for over $100 can be bought today for less than $15, and it fits in your pocket.

But calculators are no good at all when you don't have one with you, or if you do, when there's no time to reach for it. Such occasions can leave you on a limb unless you have developed the Quick Math skills explained in this chapter. Fortunately, they are relatively easy to pick up.

If your boss came to you and announced that he was raising your $17,300 annual salary to $18,455 and boasted that it was a 9 percent increase, would you thank him? Or would you quickly realize that it's more like 6⅔ percent?

Perhaps your boss is showing you some sales comparisons. Would you be able to estimate the percentage of change?

In neither case would you want to pull out a calculator. But if, on the other hand, you could voice reasonably accurate percentage figures, you'd score some big points.

Quick Math has nonbusiness benefits as well. A friend of mine tells me that while driving on an Interstate, her speedometer began to act up. It was reading too high. She didn't have time to stop and have it repaired, but she wanted to keep fairly close to the speed limit.

Most Interstates have mileage markers, so she simply

timed the next mile, driving at a speed that held the speedometer reading steady. (It read 63 mph.) The mile took 1 minute, 4 seconds. A quick calculation in her head revealed this to be a real speed of 56 mph. So she continued driving at an indicated speedometer reading of 63 mph, and was close enough to the speed limit to be ignored by the police.

There are all kinds of occasions when you need to do quick calculations but are stuck without a calculator. For example, occasions like:

* Shopping in a supermarket
* Figuring out the amount of lumber needed for a project
* Adapting recipes
* Calculating gas mileage
* Determining the amount of sales tax

Most of all, you do many calculations on your job—even if it's not a desk job and doesn't deal directly with money. The next time you report to work, keep count of the occasions in the course of your day when being able to calculate rapidly in your head would really pay off. I think the number will surprise you.

FORGET ALMOST EVERYTHING YOU EVER LEARNED ABOUT NUMBERS

You've been working with numbers most of your life—from mid-childhood on. What you've been doing, essentially, has been combining numbers in such a way that new ones are created. Nearly all of your calculations fall into one or more of the four major categories: addition, subtraction, multiplication, and division.

You may be shocked to learn that you haven't been going about it in the right way. The schools have taught you inefficient methods. These are easy to teach, but result in a lot of wasted time in the years that follow.

In fact, the school-taught methods make it nearly impossible to do even the simplest calculations in your head. The practice of adding from right to left, for example, makes paper and pencil practically a must. When you add the numbers

4783
6925

your habit has been to add the 3 and 5, then the 8 and 2, followed by the 7 and 9, and finally the 4 and 6. If you tried to do this in your head, you might arrive at the right numbers, but you'd have them in reverse order.

You're going to learn how to add more quickly from left to right, and you'll be picking up a bunch of other techniques that will give you a lifetime of benefits using Quick Math. Before we start, there are three things you should realize:

1. The majority of our daily calculations are simple enough to perform mentally, without the aid of a calculator or even pencil and paper.

2. Most of the more complicated calculations can still be handled mentally because, as you'll see, approximations are all we usually need in the way of an answer.

3. Even when a calculation is complicated enough to require pencil and paper, Quick Math can make the process much faster.

You'll be learning a lot of things you were never shown in school, and a few methods you may have been told to avoid in school. If you're at all skeptical, allow the results to speak for themselves. Give these methods a chance and see how much easier they make life for you. Even if you don't decide to use all of the methods right away, you will at least be familiar with them and know where to look in this chapter when you need them.

QUICK ADDITION

I'm about to give you a number of powerful techniques for speeding up your addition. Some appear so simple that they may fool you into doubting their effectiveness. For example, even if you learn no more than this first elementary mental technique, you'll be able to put a lot more speed in your work:

Pair your numbers so that you think of two digits as one.

This means that in a column of figures, 6 and 3 should be considered not as the two digits 6 and 3, but rather as the single digit 9. This is merely an extention of the concatenation technique you picked up for rapid reading in the last chapter, only now you are combining numbers instead of words.

On the left below is a column of figures as they appear on paper, and on the right is how you should see them.

```
6
3   9
4
2   6
```

With a little practice, you can learn to see the 6 and 3 as 9 instead of the two digits. Similarly, you'd see the 4 and 2 as 6. For now, take my word that you can easily learn to do this. Which do you think would be easier to add, the four digits in the left column, or the two digits in the right column? And think how much easier it would be to add longer columns of figures. Using this method, you could effectively cut your addition time nearly in half.

How easy is it to see pairs of digits as one digit? Try it and see for yourself. Start by practicing with the columns printed below. It may seem a bit awkward at first because it's something entirely new to you. Before long, you'll find digital concatenation becomes an automatic process in your mind. You won't even be thinking about it. You'll just be doing it.

Here are the columns of figures to work with. At this point, don't actually add the columns; practice pairing the digits.

```
3   7   2   5   4   6
2   2   1   3   1   3
8   4   9   5   7   1
1   4   0   3   1   2
7   5   8   2   4   6
1   1   1   4   4   2
1   6   2   5   3   3
4   1   3   1   3   2
```

Thus, in the left-hand column, you would "see" these

numbers: 5, 9, 8, 5. In fact, here's how you would "see" all six columns:

```
5   9   3   8   5   9
9   8   9   8   8   3
8   6   9   6   8   8
5   7   5   6   6   5
```

Practice this technique until it becomes automatic. You'll benefit from it for the rest of your life. Once you have it down pat, you're ready to move on to Part 2 of the pairing technique. Here's what Part 2 entails:

As you move down a column of figures, keep a cumulative total, adding 2 new digits at a time.

Thus, in the left-hand column above, you would first "see" the number 5. Since the next number you see is 9, you add 5 and 9 to get 14. Then you add 8, giving you 22, and finally you add 5, giving the total of 27. On the left below is the first column as it would appear to someone else; in the middle are the numbers as you see them; and on the right are the running totals that would be in your mind as you complete each calculation.

AS PRINTED	WHAT YOU SEE	RUNNING TOTAL
3		
2	5	5
8		
1	9	14
7		
1	8	22
1		
4	5	27

In working with the columns of figures above, you haven't had to combine digits totaling more than nine. But once you get the knack of pairing digits, the fact that the combination is a double-digit number (10 or more) won't make any difference to you. Practice with columns of figures such as the ones below will help:

9	3	4	7	5	6
3	7	7	4	5	4
2	4	6	7	9	3
5	9	4	3	2	4
9	7	5	3	6	2
0	2	6	5	4	8
1	9	3	5	6	3
9	1	8	5	7	9

Knowing that pairing digits—seeing two digits as one—can cut your calculating time nearly in half should provide sufficient motivation to give this simple technique the practice it deserves. Before long, you'll be doing it automatically, without giving it a conscious thought.

WHAT ABOUT LARGER NUMBERS?

"Fine," you say, "pairing digits is great when you have only a single column of digits. But what happens when each of the numbers is two or more digits long?"

You can still pair them. The technique is slightly different, but the outcome is much the same. Consider this problem:

$$\begin{array}{r} 37864 \\ +51123 \\ \hline \end{array}$$

Working from left to right, pair the top and bottom digits in each column so that you "see" just one digit. You "see" 8, 8, 9, 8, 7. And that's the sum of the two sets of numbers.

Again you have a question. "What if there's a number carry? Working from left to right doesn't allow you to carry numbers."

Fortunately, there's a means of getting around that. Consider this problem:

$$\begin{array}{r} 49 \\ +31 \\ \hline \end{array}$$

Obviously, this problem has a carry. Doing it the old-fashioned way, from right to left, you find that the 9 and 1 add to 10, leaving you with 1 to carry. If you try to do it the "new" way—from left to right—you get a 7 and a 10. Certainly 49 and 31 don't add up to 710. But think about it for a moment and you can see how you can make an easy adjustment that:

1. Allows you to add from left to right
2. Takes care of the number that is carried

Here's the rule that takes care of it for you:

When the sum of a column of figures has more than one digit, simply remove the 10's digit and add it to the preceding column.

This is what you do with the problem of adding 49 and 31 as printed above: going from left to right (pairing the top and bottom digits, of course) you "see" a 7 and a 10. Since the second column gave you an extra digit, take it away and add it to the first column. Thus the sum is 80.

As this is new to you, you might not recognize how easy—and fast—it really is. Give it a bit of practice with the problems listed below, and you'll quickly pick up the technique:

28	67	55	49	61	83
+43	+29	+46	+54	+38	+19

In the first problem, you saw a 6 and an 11. Then you merely took the first 1 from the 11 and added it to the 6, giving you a 7 and the remaining 1, or 71. In the second problem you saw an 8 and then a 16. This translated to a 96. The best part of it is that you did this mentally—no paper and pencil needed, and no going from right to left!

The third problem gives you practice with something new. You see a 9 and an 11. When you take the 1 away from the second column and add it to the first, you get a 10. Your sum is a 10 followed by the remaining 1, or 101. This is a trifle more complicated than the first two problems, granted, but still a lot quicker than taking paper and pencil and doing it the old way. Practice with some columns of figures of your own, and you'll develop proficiency in addition that you never dreamed of.

This method will be useful for you in most of the addition you are called on to do, because most of it will involve numbers of one, two, and occasionally three digits in length. But what about the longer numbers? Treat most of them in the same way. Add only the two or three most significant digits (the ones at the left). You can do this in most cases, because you rarely need precise answers. Close estimates usually suffice.

HOW TO MAKE QUICK ESTIMATES

Now you see another advantage of adding from left to right: the most important digits are on the left side. For example:

$$\$77.23$$

Here, the 77 dollars are far more important than the 23 cents. (Remember, Quick Math is for occasions when you don't have or want to use a calculator. Calculators should always be used when balancing checkbooks or updating financial journals.) In making estimates, the first two or three figures are all you normally need to use. Thus, in the problem:

$$
\begin{array}{r}
\$77.23 \\
+14.21 \\
\hline
\end{array}
$$

you could add only the 77 and the 14, or, for an even closer estimate, you could add the first three digits of each number (772 and 142). Thus, depending on the degree of accuracy you require, the estimated sum could be:

$$
\begin{array}{r}
77 \\
+14 \\
\hline
91 \\
\end{array}
$$

$$
\begin{array}{r}
77.2 \\
+14.2 \\
\hline
91.40 \\
\end{array}
$$

In either case, the sum you arrived at is within one-half of one percent. This estimating method of using a selected number of left-most digits will help you often, and in many different ways.

Let's say, for example, that you are at a discount store that has long-playing records on sale. The deal is that you can have any eight recordings for a total of $30.00. The records you've pulled from the rack carry these price tags:

$3.65
4.29
2.98
4.95
4.50
7.10
4.98
3.10

Adding up just the left-most digit of each price tells you that the records normally sell for well over $30, since the sum of that column is 31—and the cents columns haven't even been added in yet. Of course, if you wanted a closer estimate of the total, you could add the first two digits—arriving at a figure of $35.20. You know from this that your savings are substantial.

Here's some good news: If you've practiced each of the Quick-Addition techniques up to this point, you arrived at the above calculation more rapidly then you could have with a calculator in hand! Working with a calculator requires entering the digits manually—and the Quick-Addition methods you've been learning in this chapter allow you to add columns of figures in your head merely by glancing at them.

PAPER AND PENCIL ADDING MADE EASIER

There will, of course, be a few occasions when (1) you are stuck without a calculator, and (2) you need the precise sum of a series of numbers that each contain many digits. Although it's obvious that paper and pencil are required, what may not be obvious is that you don't have to do it the old way. You can still add from left to right, and do it more rapidly than by the method you were taught in school.

Here's the rule that makes it possible:

In adding each column of figures, make a small mark each time the running total reaches 10 or higher, and then continue adding as if the total were smaller by ten.

Thus, if you add 9 and 7, you arrive at 16. Make a small mark on the paper and convert your running total to 6, instead

of 16. Let's do it with a single column of figures, to make it easy
to understand. Each time you arrive at 10 or more, make a
small dot immediately to the left of the digit where it occurred.
To make the example as simple as possible, we'll add each
digit individually, instead of the recommended two at a time.

$$
\begin{array}{c}
9 \\
.7 \\
3 \\
.4 \\
1 \\
2
\end{array}
$$

In the above example, 9+7=16. Put a mark next to the 7,
and think of your running total as 6. 6+3=9. 9+4=13. Put a mark
next to the 4 and think of your running total as 3. 3+1=4. 4+2=6.
Your total is 6 preceded by 2 dots, and that means it's 26.

Although the step-by-step explanation you've just read
may make it appear like an involved process, it really isn't.
With practice, you'll find it much speedier than the old-fashioned
way.

Here's the same method employed with larger numbers:

$$
\begin{array}{r}
4\,3\,7\,8 \\
2\,4.9.3 \\
1\,0.9\,2 \\
.7.8\,1\,1 \\
.6\,3\,0.9 \\
\underline{2.4.9\,3} \\
2\,2\,5\,6
\end{array}
$$

In the first step, above, you have added each column of
figures, making a dot whenever the running total has reached
10 or more, and then proceeding as if the total were its second
digit (for example, 4 instead of 14).

In the second step, you write in the number of dots for
each column, making sure to offset it one column to the left.
Then simply add the number of dots to the preliminary total:

$$
\begin{array}{r}
4\,3\,7\,8 \\
2\,4.9.3 \\
1\,0.9\,2 \\
.7.8\,1\,1
\end{array}
$$

```
            .6 3 0.9
            2.4.9 3
            2 2 5 6   (preliminary total)
            2 2 3 2   (number of dots)
            2 4 5 7 6  (grand total)
```

You've seen some powerful time-savers for the quick addition of figures, presented in a logical order for you to learn and practice with. Perhaps by now your head is swimming with new information, so let's review the techniques you can use to speed up the process of adding numbers:

1. Always add from left to right, adding the left-most column of figures first and then moving to the next column to the right.

2. In adding a column of figures, pair the numbers so that you think of two digits as one.

3. As you move down a column of figures, keep a cumulative total, adding two new digits at a time.

4. When the sum of a column of figures has more than one digit, remove the 10's digit and add it to the preceding column.

5. Get in the habit of making quick estimates in the majority of instances when precise sums are not needed. Depending on the degree of accuracy you need, add the 1, 2, or 3 most significant columns (the ones at the left).

6. When precise answers are absolutely required, use the "dot" method of paper and pencil addition.

There's still a valuable tip to come on Quick Addition. It's being saved until later because it deals with all kinds of calculations, not just addition. It involves a speedy way of checking your answers.

QUICK SUBTRACTION

Doing subtraction without the aid of a calculator is an easy matter, and again it's done from left to right.

You saw that the main problem complicating things in addition was the need to carry numbers. In subtraction, it's just the opposite: borrowing. Subtraction from left to right is child's play when no borrowing is required, as in the following examples:

$$\begin{array}{r} 78 \\ -23 \\ \hline \end{array} \qquad \begin{array}{r} 54976489 \\ -41753126 \\ \hline \end{array}$$

Merely proceed from the left, subtracting each digit from the one above it, and you have your solution. Unfortunately, most problems are not so simple. Consider this one:

$$\begin{array}{r} 62 \\ -48 \\ \hline \end{array}$$

Subtracting the 4 from the 6 goes well, but then we're faced with subtracting an 8 from a 2. It may surprise you to learn that there are two easy ways to deal with it. One is mental, and the other requires paper and pencil. Both are much shorter than the methods you learned in school.

The mental method: Add enough to the bottom number so that it ends in 0. Then add the same amount to the top number. This leaves you without any need to borrow, and you can easily subtract from left to right. In the above example, 48 would become 50, and 62 becomes 64. Then it's an easy matter to subtract 50 from 64. Here are four problems, each printed two ways. In each example, the original form is shown at the left and the adjusted form on the right:

$$\begin{array}{rr} 72 & 73 \\ -19 & -20 \\ \hline \end{array} \qquad \begin{array}{rr} 63 & 65 \\ -28 & -30 \\ \hline \end{array} \qquad \begin{array}{rr} 52 & 54 \\ -38 & -40 \\ \hline \end{array} \qquad \begin{array}{rr} 84 & 85 \\ -29 & -30 \\ \hline \end{array}$$

This is called the mental method for the obvious reason that it can be done in your head, it's so simple. You'll be able to use it often, because much of the subtracting we do consists of numbers no longer than two digits—or numbers can be shortened to that length when total precision is not required and an estimate will suffice. The mental method often works with numbers that are three digits in length, but for most longer numbers, the paper and pencil method is best.

The paper and pencil method: Subtract from left to right, as before. When you need to borrow a number (such as subtracting an 8 from a 5) do as you always have done. Subtract 8 from 15. After writing the answer down (in this case, 7) put a slash through the number located immediately to the left. Here's what it would look like:

$$
\begin{array}{r}
557 \\
-384 \\
\hline
\not{2}73
\end{array}
$$

A slash through a number tells you that it is to be read as if it were actually one number less than what it says. The solution above, then, would be 173, instead of 273. In other words, whenever you see a slash, subtract 1 from the number. Most people become so much at home with this method that they never actually write in the corrected figures; they "see" a 2 having a slash in it as a 1, and an 8 as a 7.

Here are some more problems to practice with. You'll find that practice enables you to handle them with more speed (and probably even more accuracy) than the old school-taught backwards method. Remember as you practice with these problems that whenever you need to borrow a number, you should draw a slash through the number located immediately to the left. The left-most problem already has the slash drawn in, to serve as a guide for you.

$$
\begin{array}{rrrrrrrrr}
7845 & 6382 & 7295 & 9923 & 7711 & 8320 & 5936 & 6021 & 8246 \\
-5932 & -4293 & -7186 & -8947 & -1845 & -5603 & -3677 & -5441 & -6739 \\
\hline
\not{2}913
\end{array}
$$

The solution to the left-most problem is, of course, read as 1913, because the 2 has a slash through it.

THE SPEED FACTOR

There's a good reason why people who are adept at the Quick-Addition and Quick-Subtraction methods (as I trust you will soon become) can often do their figuring faster without a calculator than they can with one. They save the time it takes to make keystrokes on the calculator.

The number of steps required to do the work mentally is often fewer than the number of manual keystrokes that have to be made if using a calculator. A simple example is adding 3+2. Only one mental calculation is involved, but four keystrokes must be made on the calculator (3,+,2,=).

When it comes to multiplication and division, however, the number of mental calculations often exceeds what's required with a calculator. As an example, here's an elementary multiplication problem:

$$
\begin{array}{r}
40 \\
\times 32 \\
\hline
80 \\
120 \\
\hline
1280
\end{array}
$$

Six keystrokes are required to do this problem with a calculator (entering each of the digits, entering the multiplication key, and entering the equals key). Eight steps are required when you do it without a calculator, and that's assuming the initial problem has already been written on paper.

Does this mean that there are no speedy methods to do multiplication and division without a calculator? Not at all. For many of the problems that you're called on to do each day, there are indeed some rapid techniques.

QUICK MULTIPLICATION

You're going to learn two quick-and-easy methods that will allow you to do a great many multiplication problems in your head—no paper and pencil required. The first involves removing and then replacing 0's. For example, can you tell me within a few seconds what 400 × 700 comes to? If you're like most people, you can't.

But certainly you know that 4×7 is 28. And that's the key to solving 400 × 700. Here's where you do:

1. Remove the 0's.
2. Multiply the stripped-down numbers.
3. Tack the removed 0's on to the end of your answer.

The original problem, 400 × 700, had four 0's. So, after you multiply 4 × 7 and arrive at 28, you tack on four 0's, which gives you 280,000. There's one thing to be careful about. If multiplying the stripped-down numbers gives you an initial answer that ends in 0, any 0's that you previously removed must be tacked back on to the right of that existing 0. In other words, if the problem was 40 × 50, you'd first remove two 0's, then multiply 4 × 5 to arrive at 20, and then replace the original 0's, converting 20 to your final answer of 2,000.

Work with these practice problems:

20	450	3000	120	130	1500	2000	700	1100
×40	× 20	× 300	× 20	×300	×3000	× 400	× 70	× 30

You can see that it doesn't take much practice to become adept at this kind of multiplication. Before long, you should be able to do similar problems without even seeing them on paper. If someone asks you what 2,000 × 400 is, you'll know almost immediately that it's 800,000.

What happens when neither of the numbers to be multiplied ends in 0? What do you do with a number such as 43 × 11? You change one of the numbers so that it does end in 0.

Pick whichever number is closest to having a 0 at the end. In the above example, the 11 is only 1 digit away from 10. The next step is to multiply the other number by the number that now ends in 0. In this case, 10 × 43 = 430. Since we were really supposed to multiply by 11 instead of 10, we'll add another 43 to the answer we got. 430 + 43 = 473. And that's the answer to our problem. Here, in step-by-step form, is the procedure:

1. Choose the number that is closest to having a 0 at the end, and adjust it by adding or subtracting just enough to give it a 0 ending. (11 becomes 10)

2. Multiply the other number by the adjusted number. (10 × 43 = 430)

3. Compensate for the original adjustment you made by adding or subtracting to your interim solution. (430 + 43 = 473)

You'll see that when you reduce a number in order to give it a 0 ending, you'll have to add at the end of the problem. When you enlarge a number to bring it up to a 0 ending, you'll have to subtract later. If, for example, our problem was 9 × 34, we'd change the 9 to a 10 and arrive at 340. But then we'd have to subtract 34, showing the answer to be 306.

If the problem was 8 × 38, our interim solution would be 380. But then we'd subtract 2 × 38 to compensate. 380 − 76 = 304. Consider these typical problems:

44	56	31	17	29	45	66	84	75	88
×11	× 9	×25	×29	×15	×19	×78	×11	×21	×12

Thus, you can see that mental multiplication is not only possible, but easily done when the problems have numbers that end in 0 or that can be altered to end in 0. Certainly, there are many problems that don't fit these molds—but you have learned powerful techniques that will handle much of your multiplication.

QUICK DIVISION

Think about it for a moment, and you'll realize that you have already learned how to divide more quickly. Think about the kinds of steps you take to solve a problem such as this:

$$
\begin{array}{r}
168 \\
43\overline{)7224} \\
43 \\
\hline
292 \\
258 \\
\hline
344 \\
344 \\
\end{array}
$$

Doing long division involves (1) estimating and (2) subtractions. In the above problem, you begin by estimating how many times 43 goes into 72 (1). Then you subtract 43 from 72 and bring down one more digit (292). The process of estimating and subtracting continues until you arrive at your solution.

You've already learned that the secret of estimating is to shorten the numbers. Looking at the above example again, estimating how many times 43 goes into 258 is made easier by cutting one digit from each number: 4 into 25 gives you 6.

What you've learned about Quick Subtraction helps you with the only other type of calculation required for division. Going from left to right, you can rapidly subtract 258 from 292, or subtract any other numbers you may encounter.

The only requirements for Quick Division are skills you've already learned in this chapter. Go back over the sections on estimating and on Quick Subtraction; become proficient in these, and you'll be skilled at Quick Division.

HOW TO SAVE NEARLY HALF YOUR CALCULATING TIME

We were taught in school that when we do calculations with paper and pencil, we must do them over again to check the answer. If, for example, you added a column of figures, you were supposed to add it in reverse order to see if you would arrive at the same total. If you did a problem in division, you were supposed to multiply the answer by the divisor. In multiplication, you put the bottom number on the top and the top number on the bottom—and then started multiplying all over again.

Naturally, this checking doubled the time it took to complete a problem. Therefore, it stands to reason that if we can drastically cut the checking time we can greatly reduce the overall time it takes to complete the problem. And, fortunately, we can.

The way to do it is to shorten the number of figures that must be checked. Let's say we have just added a column of ten numbers, each of which was 5 digits long. In the old-fashioned way of checking, we'd have to add again a total of 50 digits. But with the method you're about to learn, you'd only have to add 10 digits.

What you will be adding are the sums of the digits contained on each line. And that'll be just one digit long instead of the original five. When you learn how to figure the digit sum, you can use it to check any problem—whether it's addition, subtraction, multiplication, or division.

Here's something you should know:

The Digit Sum Method is so quick, many people even use it to check solutions they've obtained on a calculator!

There's usually no way to be absolutely sure you've entered all of the figures correctly in a hand-held calculator, since most models don't have a paper tape to check. The only valid verification method is doing the problem all over again—or, as you'll see, using the Digit Sum Method.

First, you'll be shown how to ascertain digit sums quickly and easily. And then you'll see how to apply them to any problem.

HOW TO DETERMINE DIGIT SUMS

The simplest explanation for digit sum is that it is the sum of all the digits in a number. The digit sum of 31 would be 4, since $3 + 1 = 4$.

But you need to know a bit more than this. If the digit sum is itself more than 1 digit in length (say 12), then the final answer is the sum of that number (in this case, 3). As an example, let's consider the number 343214. The digits add up to 17, and this, in turn, adds up to 8. Thus the digit sum of 343214 is 8.

With a little practice, you can do digit sum work rapidly, and here's a tip to help you go even faster: Ignore 9's. Whenever a 9 appears in the number, pay no attention to it. Whenever your running total reaches 9, consider that you're back at 0.

Here's why this works. Consider the number 94. The sum of the digits is 4. That's because $9 + 4 = 13$, and $1 + 3 = 4$. If you had ignored the 9 in the first place, you would have arrived at the same 4. Now let's see how this works in a longer number. In 457 the digit sum is 7 $(4 + 5 = 9; 9 + 7 = 16; 1 + 6 = 7)$. We could have arrived at the same answer by ignoring the $4 + 5$, since they add up to 9. The remaining digit is 7.

But what happens when the digit total itself adds up to 9 (as in 387)? Again, consider it a 0.

Please take some time right now to practice arriving at sums of digits. Simply write down on a sheet of paper a variety of numbers and the sums of their digits. You'll see how easy it is to become both speedy and proficient.

Now, assuming you fully understand how to arrive at digit sums, here's how you can use them to prove your mathematical calculations.

QUICK PROOF OF ADDITION

To prove an addition problem, check to see if the sum of all the digit sums equals the digit sum of the total. Examine this example:

Numbers	Digit Sums
437	5
285	6
+164	2
886	4

The answer checks out, because the digit sum of the total equals the sum of all the digit sums. You don't actually have to write the digit sums out, as was done above. You can keep a running total in your mind, adding the sums as you proceed down the list of numbers. Just remember that when your running total happens to hit 9, consider it a 0.

Thus, in the column of figures above, your mental process would be as follows: $4 + 3 = 7; 7 + 7 = 14 = 5; 5 + 2 = 7; 7 + 8 = 15 = 6; 6 + 5 = 11 = 2; 2 + 1 = 3; 3 + 6 = 9 = 0; 0 + 4 = 4.$

On paper, it looks involved. Doing it in your head, it's a breeze. Try it! You'll be amazed at how rapidly you can check long columns of figures.

Is it foolproof? Not quite. There are some types of errors that it won't catch. An example is when two digits on the same line become transposed. Also, it wouldn't catch an instance in which you've written down a 9 in your answer instead of 0, or vice versa. But the system is 99.44 percent pure, and a lot of knowledgeable people count on it as a valuable and accurate time-saver.

QUICK PROOF OF SUBTRACTION

As you know, the school-taught way to check subtraction is to add the answer to the number that was subtracted. This is supposed to equal the number that was subtracted from.

The Digit Sum Method does the same thing. Add the digit sum of the answer to the digit sum of the number that was subtracted. This should equal the digit sum of the number that was subtracted from. Here's an example:

Numbers	Digit Sum
537	6
−241	7
296	8

You can see that the problem checks out because the digit sums check out. The digit sum of the answer is 8. Add that to 7 and you get 15, which translates to 6. And 6 is the digit sum of the number that was subtracted from.

QUICK PROOF OF MULTIPLICATION

Multiply the digit sums of the two numbers you multiplied. When this is reduced to a single digit it should be equal to the digit sum of the answer. Here's a demonstration problem:

Numbers	Digit Sum
437	5
× 24	×6
10,488	3

Multiplying the digit sums of the numbers in the problem gives you 30, which translates to 3, and that is equal to the digit sum of the solution, so it checks out.

QUICK PROOF OF DIVISION

In division, you were taught in school to check the answer by multiplying it by the number you divided by. If this equaled the number that was divided, you had the right answer.

$$\frac{81}{4)\,324}$$

Since $81 \times 4 = 324$, the answer checks out.

The Digit Sum Method is the same, except that you are dealing with digit sums instead of full numbers. You check the above problem by multiplying the digit sum of 4 (4) by the digit sum of 81 (0, since 9 translates to 0) and obtain 0. This equals the digit sum of the number that was divided (324 adds up to 9, which translates to 0).

Of course, in division we sometimes have remainders. Suppose we divide 325 by 4. Our answer in that case is 4, with 1 as a remainder. Check it out just as you did before, multiplying digit sums of the answer and the number you divided by. Then add the remainder. This should be the same as the digit sum of the number you divided by.

Spend some time getting accustomed to Digit Sums. Like many other people, you'll find:

1. Although it has taken several pages to explain, the Digit Sum Method is remarkably simple.

2. You'll develop the ability to determine the digit sum of a number almost as fast as you can read the number itself.

3. You can check solutions using the Digit Sum Method in about one-tenth the time it took to do the original problem.

Here is something worth remembering: Even if during the first reading of this chapter you did not practice each of the Quick Math techniques, you can learn them at any time. This chapter will always be here to show you how. The important thing is that now you know there are quicker and better ways to do routine calculating. When you're ready for them, they're here waiting for you.

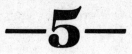

How to
Solve Problems
That Stump Other People

You're about to learn an uncommon means of solving problems. It's not the way most people seek solutions—but then, most people are not nearly as good at problem solving as they should be.

The world's most successful people have achieved success largely because they know how to tackle problems that hold their competitors back. These same problem-solving techniques are available to you. They'll enable you to see solutions that your colleagues miss entirely, and you'll be rewarded for it.

WHAT PROBLEM SOLVING CAN DO FOR YOU

The problem-solving techniques described in this and later chapters have worked wonders for successful people in all walks of life. Having spent much of my career working with, interviewing, and counseling top achievers, I've made note of their special abilities—and you can be sure that solving problems was at the top of the list.

Studying the careers and life styles of these people has revealed to me the techniques that you'll find presented in this book. What these techniques have done for others, they can do for you. They can:

* Enable you to face problems squarely and defeat them easily
* Mark you as a person of leadership and foresight because you take action while others are still in the "worrying" stage
* Bring rapid progress in your job, resulting in frequent promotions and salary increases
* Heighten your success potential in business because of greater ability to deal with obstacles that slow down your competitors

ELIMINATE THE TWO BARRIERS THAT CONFUSE MOST PEOPLE

When I tell people that there are better ways to solve problems than the methods they've been using, the typical reply is, "Who needs a better way to solve problems? I'm getting along just fine."

What these people don't realize, and what you may not realize, is that if you go about trying to solve tough problems using conventional methods, the odds are stacked against you.

There are two barriers standing in your way:

1. Misinformation
2. Incorrect focus

You'll see just how significant these barriers can be. We're going to examine them individually, showing how you can overcome them. Then we'll move on to a powerful means of conquering almost any problem that confronts you.

ELIMINATE THE FIRST BARRIER: CORRECT THE MISINFORMATION AND SOLVE THE UNSOLVABLE

Most people wouldn't dream of solving an arithmetic problem by majority vote—but it's amazing how many other problems they try to solve that way. If you needed to know the sum of a column of figures, and four people told you it was 4,397 while another person claimed it was 4,398, you probably wouldn't accept either answer as correct. Instead, you'd add the figures yourself.

But when it comes to other types of problems, we happily swallow information handed us by other people without checking the facts—and then wonder why we aren't making much headway. When your facts aren't correct, you either can't solve the problem or it's going to take you a lot longer.

One of the Sunday newspapers that I read carries a puzzle consisting of a diagram of a chess board and the location of the various pieces after a number of moves have been made. The reader is challenged to study this "game in progress" and determine how to win it in two moves (known as a "mate in two").

I spent more than an hour on a recent Sunday unable to find any way in which the game could be won in two moves. Going through all the conceivable moves, I could find no solution. Even getting out my chess board and setting up the pieces the way they were printed in the diagram was no help.

Finally, in frustration, I looked at the solution printed at the bottom of the page. It was immediately obvious that the diagram of the board as presented in the puzzle had been incorrect. One piece had been printed in the wrong square. Misinformation had made the puzzle unsolvable.

In real-life problems, the answer isn't printed at the bottom of the page. Some people go on for hours, days, or weeks working on the basis of misinformation.

THREE PROBLEM-SOLVING EXAMPLES

When people say something is impossible, they are basing their assumption on whatever information they have at hand. Some or all of that information may be incorrect. The person who comes along with the right information may easily accomplish what others thought impossible.

The ability to solve difficult or even "unsolvable" problems by replacing misinformation with facts has been a big boost in the lives and careers of many people. Here are some examples of what this kind of problem solving has done:

* Stan E. lived in an area where heavy salting of the roads
  during the winter created a major rust problem affecting
  cars and trucks. People accepted rust as inevitable. But
  Stan, the owner of a taxi fleet, had no rust problems at
  all. How come? Stan did not share the misinformation
  that guided most other people. He knew better than to
  believe the theory that most rusting occurs during the
  winter. He knew that for every ten degrees the tempera-
  ture climbs above freezing, the rate of oxidation doubles.
  This is important, because oxidation is the process that
  causes rust. Most people in salty areas wash their cars
  frequently in the winter, but neglect to do so the rest of
  the year. By having his cars thoroughly rinsed in the
  spring and summer months, Stan eliminated the rust
  problem.

* At a time when the skyrocketing cost of buying and financing a home convinced many young couples that
  there was no chance of escaping apartment life, Joel
  and Grace N. found a way. Most other couples were
  burdened by the misinformation that sophisticated
  trading techniques are available only to the well-to-do.
  But Joel and Grace knew that the same kind of wheeling
  and dealing employed by big real estate entrepreneurs
  can be used by private home buyers. They were able to
  solve their home-buying problem and obtain a lovely
  residence on a half-acre plot. The home had originally
  stood on a full acre of land. Joel and Grace worked out a
  deal to buy the full acre and have the broker sign up
  buyers for two quarter-acre plots that were sliced from
  the property. The money that Joel and Grace received
  for the extra land more than covered their down payment.

* Roger W., the bookkeeper for a construction outfit, was
  able to keep the company from going bankrupt by developing a new source of income. The firm owned a lot
  of heavy equipment, some of it standing idle much of
  the time. The owner was saddled with the misinformation that there was no profitable use for equipment
  that wasn't currently needed. Roger suggested renting
  it out to other firms on a daily or weekly basis. This
  solved the company's cash-flow problem and led to

Roger's being promoted to general manager of the company.

Each of these people solved seemingly hopeless problems by dealing with them in ways that other people hadn't thought of. There is nothing particularly brilliant about any of the solutions. It's just that misinformation had clouded the vision of people who might otherwise have been able to see them.

KNOW THE SOURCES OF MISINFORMATION

Many of the techniques in this book were developed by highly successful businessmen and businesswomen. The commercial world is tough, and these people have had to use Mental Leverage in order to survive. With competition so keen, there is little room for mistakes—and no room at all for misinformation.

The kind of business people we're talking about have this in common: they check out facts for themselves. Experience has taught them how expensive misinformation can be.

The president of a tool manufacturing company spoke about misinformation at a recent management seminar, and in his talk he listed some of the major sources of misinformation he had encountered:

* "Facts" from people who have a personal stake in the matter
* Observations of people who have little training or experience in that particular field
* Hastily prepared data that may have typographical and numerical errors
* Superficial reports that don't go thoroughly into the subject
* Preconceived notions that were never right in the first place

The tool company executive explained that whenever he's confronted with a problem, the first thing he does is reexamine the facts. Which facts are indisputable? Which might be questioned? What information is missing?

"You may surprise yourself," he said, "and find there is really no problem at all. Misinformation—and missing information—may have misled you into believing there's a problem where none actually exists."

Perhaps you have experienced this sort of thing in balancing your checkbook. At first glance it seems as if you've overdrawn your account, but a careful check of the entries shows that you failed to record a deposit and that you really have a healthy balance.

Even if the information verifies that a problem does, indeed, exist, you are a step ahead of the game by verifying the key facts. As you'll see later in this chapter, having the facts provides you with the basis for charting an easy course from problem to solution.

Thus, Rule Number 1 in problem solving is this:

> Recheck the facts to (a) determine if the problem really does exist, and (b) provide a solid foundation for solving it.

The people who face challenging problems almost every day have it down to a science. Clearing out misinformation is the first rule of that science.

ELIMINATE THE SECOND BARRIER: FOCUS ON THE DESIRED OUTCOME

When a problem suddenly crops up, it's human nature to become so concerned with the problem itself that you forget it was merely an obstacle in the path toward a goal. You start paying so much attention to the obstacle that you lose sight of the goal it's preventing you from achieving.

When successful problem solvers are faced with an obstacle, they look beyond it to the goal they are seeking—and then examine various ways of achieving that goal. Often they find that there really isn't much of a problem at all, because it can easily be bypassed.

Just think, for example, of the great many excellent business ideas that must have gone down the drain because their originators couldn't find adequate financing. It's an obstacle that has nipped many a potential wealth-building idea in the bud.

The usual source of financial backing for a business is, of course, the friendly local bank. Unfortunately, thousands of people have discovered just how unfriendly a bank can be when they seek a business loan to finance their money-making schemes.

Bankers, it seems, frown on lending money for unproven ideas. If you can show that your plan has already been tried and proven, you may get the loan. But without cash to get your plan rolling, how can you prove it works? For many people it's a vicious cycle, and eventually many of them give up. But not the woman I'm going to tell you about.

WHEN THE CONVENTIONAL ROUTE FAILS

Pamela S. was a young widow with an idea. The trouble is, the idea was going to cost her $20,000 that she didn't have. Pam's idea was to lease computer terminals to professional people who wished to tie in with data banks. The terminals would allow lawyers, for instance, to gain access to law libraries far more comprehensive than their own. Stock market and commodity investors could obtain up-to-the-minute prices in their homes or offices.

"Merely by typing a few letters on the terminal, my clients would be able to get information that otherwise would be much more difficult to obtain," Pam explains. "To get started in this business, I needed several terminals, and some front money to pay for advertising and start-up costs. With my professional background in data processing, I thought it would be a cinch to get a business loan. Was I surprised!"

Pam was turned down by one bank after another. She doesn't know if it was because she's a woman or simply the fact that although she was experienced with computers she had not proven herself as an entrepreneur. At any rate, she had no success following the conventional route, seeking the type of business loan that anyone with such an idea would seek.

"Suddenly it dawned on me," Pam recalls, "that I was concentrating so much on getting a business loan that I had made THAT my goal ... instead of realizing that my real goal was to get hold of $20,000 to finance a business. It didn't really matter what the borrowing method was, as long as I got the money."

Realizing this, Pam began thinking of various alternatives until she arrived at the easiest one of all—increasing the mortgage on her home. The home's value had shot up tremendously, and she found that the bank holding the mortgage was more than willing to increase it by the $20,000 she needed.

USE A "TELEPHOTO LENS"

This experience taught Pam a lesson that has continued to benefit her throughout the development and expansion of her highly successful business.

"Whenever a problem crops up," she says, "I get out my telephoto lens. Not a real lens, of course. What I mean is that I focus on the long-range goal rather than the immediate obstruction. Invariably I find a simple means of getting around the problem at hand."

I've found that successful people in all walks of life do this, while failures are loaded with excuses about problems that have prevented them from getting ahead. So here's Rule Number 2 in problem solving:

> Set your sights on the long-range goal and examine alternative ways of reaching it.

This may seem as if you're avoiding the immediate problem, but why not? The world's most successful people have found that the easiest way to solve a problem is to find a means of getting around it.

HOW TO ACTIVATE ALL YOUR MENTAL RESOURCES

When you're faced with a thorny problem that defies all attempts at an easy solution, you've got to marshal your full mental powers. This puts people who understand and utilize Mental Leverage at a distinct advantage. They have more resources at their command than other people.

The problem-solving system described in this chapter increases the power of these mental weapons:

* Your conscious reasoning skills
* Your subconscious solution-finding ability
* Your talent to unravel problems through visualization

By applying these three mental weapons, you'll be charting an easy course from problem to solution. But before I explain how to go about it, it's important that you know why the system works.

TOOLS THAT STRENGTHEN YOUR CONSCIOUS REASONING SKILLS

When you are faced with a problem, you probably do one or more of the following:

1. Mull it over in your mind.
2. Discuss it with associates.
3. Use trial and error to find a solution.

These are the standard problem-solving techniques, and sometimes they work. Although they're fine as far as they go, they fail to utilize a good deal of your reasoning power. Such simple tools as paper, pencil, and a cassette tape recorder can leverage a lot more of your reasoning power.

As you may have gathered, one of the problem-solving techniques outlined in this chapter will have you charting your solution on paper. You'll be listing the problem, and then as you discover the steps needed for its solution, you'll be writing them down as well. Most people write things on paper so they won't forget them. Your motive will be different.

Psychologists have discovered (and so have business problem solvers) that the human mind is much more orderly when it has something tangible to work with. Your mind can wander in a thousand different directions as you puzzle over a problem, but if you must put the problem on paper, you are forced to concentrate on that one item alone. And as you follow the path I'm going to lay out for you in uncovering the solution, the orderly reasoning process will become even more efficient.

People who must frequently face problems find that carrying a tiny microcassette recorder can be a great help. One such person is Ed J., who manages an advertising specialty business.

"My work is so hectic that I often get interrupted after starting to chart a problem and its solution," Ed explains. "Laying the problem aside, I go on to other things. Then hours or even days later I may be struck with an idea for dealing with the problem. Some of my best thoughts, for example, occur while I'm driving. I carry a pocket-sized tape recorder clipped to my belt, and it's a simple matter to record my thoughts before they're forgotten.

"I bought the machine for dictating letters, but I'm actually using it a lot more to keep a record of ideas that might otherwise be lost. Then, when I get back to the office, I listen to the tape and enter the new ideas on the chart."

HOW YOUR SUBCONSCIOUS HELPS SOLVE PROBLEMS

When you start to chart a problem, you are not only putting it on paper, you're also sending a message to your subconscious mind. You are, in effect, telling it to get busy with the problem even after your conscious mind has turned to other matters.

Because it is indeed subconscious, we're not aware of all that is going on in this "hidden" mind that each of us has. Nor are we aware of its great power to help resolve our problems. And certainly most people don't know how to tap this tremendous mental resource.

A psychology professor friend of mine likens the human mind to an iceberg.

"Three-quarters of an iceberg floats under the surface of the water," he notes, "and only one-quarter is visible above the water. Think of that visible part as your conscious mind—the part that reasons for you. And think of the submerged part as your subconscious mind. It's three times as large, and it may be three times as important."

Most people have heard about some of the wonderful things the subconscious mind can do, but few are familiar with its potential role in solving problems. They don't know that practitioners of Mental Leverage—the people who get the most from their minds and become big achievers—make full use of their subconscious problem-solving ability.

Here are some things you should know about the sub-conscious:

* It is subject to suggestion. This means it will accept almost any thought you give it. Unlike your conscious mind, it is not controlled by reason, so it doesn't argue with what you tell it. If, for example, you repeatedly say to yourself, "I am a multimillionaire," your subconscious will believe it even though your conscious mind knows it's not true. Some people liken it to hypnosis; when a hypnotist tells a person that he is extremely cold, that person starts to shiver. Hypnosis functions at the subconscious level, but you don't need to be hypnotized to utilize the subconscious.

* Your brain stores enough information to fill 90,000,000 books. Somewhere, buried in all that information, are the solutions to nearly every problem you are likely to face. Unfortunately, only a small portion of this data is readily available to your conscious mind.

* When you are stumped by a problem, you can "tell" your subconscious that somewhere within the depths of your mind there are ideas that will lead to a workable solution. Then, as you go about your other business, your subconscious will search through your memory for ideas and events matching the current circumstances. It will present to your conscious mind information that you would never have recalled otherwise.

Using your subconscious in this manner is similar to the many times that you have had a certain word or name "on the tip of your tongue" but couldn't quite think of it. After struggling to recall it, you have eventually given up. Then, hours or maybe even days later, while you are not even thinking of the subject, the word or name comes to you in a flash. That's your sub-conscious in action. You knew the information was buried in your mind somewhere, but you couldn't quite get it out. So your subconscious retrieved it for you.

Please remember that at this point I'm not telling you HOW to use your subconscious as an aid in solving problems;

I'm merely telling you WHY it works. The actual instructions come a bit later.

SAVE HOURS OF PAINSTAKING EFFORT

Walter M. uses his subconscious as a working tool in his job as the production manager for an electronics manufacturing firm.

"When things go wrong here, they go wrong with a vengeance," Walt says. "Our products are each composed of dozens of smaller components that we buy from outside suppliers. If just one of those suppliers fails to ship the components to us on schedule, an entire production run can be halted.

"It's my job to keep the assembly lines going, and you can imagine what I go through when parts are missing. I either have to locate them somewhere else, or reschedule production for some other product that doesn't require that particular component. Meanwhile, the people we sell to are expecting us to stick to the shipping schedule we promised.

"It's like a jigsaw puzzle. You've got to fit all the pieces together to keep the factory busy, your customers happy, and the products rolling off the line. Sometimes it can be mighty hard to get all the pieces together in the right combination.

"That's when I call on my subconscious. I know, deep down, that by juggling things around there is a way to meet all the requirements. But it can take hours and hours of painstaking trial-and-error paper work to make all the pieces fit together. What I often do instead is let my subconscious come up with the answers for me.

"If a problem is particularly perplexing, I set it aside for a while, knowing that there is a way to solve it, and that way will come to me. Then I relax my mind and start doing other work. Before long—usually the same day, but within twenty-four hours at the most—all kinds of solutions start entering my mind. They often 'arrive' at moments when I least expect them.

"As each solution hits me, I write it down or record it on my cassette. Then, when I have an opportunity, I get out my problem chart and begin to see which solutions will fit, and where. Almost invariably, the answers I need are there, and things work out smoothly."

YOUR TALENT TO UNRAVEL PROBLEMS THROUGH VISUALIZATION

Visualization uses the best of both worlds. It combines the benefits of your conscious and subconscious minds. When you visualize the solution to a problem, you are doing so consciously, but many of the thoughts and ideas that come to you are drawn from the subconscious level.

The visualization problem-solving method to be outlined here is not infallible. There are times when it simply doesn't produce any results. But it is so easy to do, and takes such little time, that it's always worth a try. Here's what you do:

1. Go to a quiet area where you won't be disturbed.

2. Think of the best possible outcome of the problem you are currently faced with. Obviously you don't know yet how it will be resolved, but you do know the desired outcome. Picture this in your mind as vividly as you can.

3. Now go backwards a step at a time. First you have pictured the outcome; next visualize what happened just before the problem was resolved. What was the final step that brought the solution? And what happened just before that . . . and before that? Keep going back in time, visualizing each stage of the solution's unfoldment. Before long, you should have the entire solution visualized.

The reason this type of visualization often works in solving problems is that your subconscious is being forced into immediate action. Normally, the subconscious takes its own sweet time in delivering the information you seek from it. That's why the usual method of seeking its help is, as mentioned earlier, to relax your mind, turn to other matters, and wait for the right ideas to surface.

The Reverse Motion Visualization Technique calls your imagination into play, and imagination is closely related to the subconscious. People often find that as they visualize in the reverse order of events, their subconscious feeds a steady stream of ideas to keep the reverse motion going. Before long, they have the whole problem worked out.

Let's consider a simple example to see how this works. The problem is that your boss is coming to dinner tonight, and because you napped longer than you intended, there won't be time to cook the roast you planned. But it's the only meat in the house, and you're stuck without a main course.

> Using Reverse Motion Visualization, you calm your mind, sit down in a quiet room, and begin to picture your boss enjoying a wonderful roast at your dining room table. Then, bit by bit, you move backwards in time. How did the roast get there? You carried it to the table. But if there wasn't time to cook it, how did it get cooked? Certainly not in your oven . . . but how about a microwave oven? There would have been time for that. All right, it was cooked by microwave, but where did the oven come from? Did you go out and buy one? No, there wasn't time. You borrowed one, that's what you did! Your neighbor, Sally, has been boasting about how great hers is. You borrowed it from her, and Sally was eager to show you how to use it.

And there you have a feasible solution to your problem. It probably took less than five minutes to achieve. You probably would not have thought of it in time if you had tried to puzzle out a solution in the normal way, from beginning to end. Reverse Motion Visualization, marshalling the combined forces of your conscious and subconscious minds, scored the victory for you.

The technique works enough of the time to warrant giving it a try whenever you're perlexed by a problem. If, however, you continue to be stumped, then charting is your answer. As you'll see, there will still be opportunities to use your subconscious.

HOW TO MAKE A TOUGH PROBLEM MUCH EASIER

Making a tough problem easy is right down Barry R.'s alley. After all, he did something most other people would never dream of tackling: he started a bank from scratch. I tell about Barry's achievement in my recent book, *Control Dynamics for Mastery Over People*, published by Parker Publishing Co., Inc., West Nyack, N.Y.

Barry spotted the need for a bank in the rapidly growing community where he lived. His only experience in banking was a brief period as a teller and then as a loan officer soon after graduating from college. He's the first to admit that the idea of starting a new bank overwhelmed him until he read a magazine article outlining the charting method that you, too, are about to learn.

Barry's problem—starting a bank—was something he had never done before and that many people might say he was not qualified to do. It was, obviously, as big a problem as most of us are ever likely to encounter. He did it by dividing a big job into smaller, more workable chunks. Taking paper and pencil, he listed each of the steps involved in creating a new bank, knowing that a complex task suddenly becomes much easier when you take it one step at a time.

The first thing Barry did was to write down his problem:

> To establish a local bank, filling a need that now exists in this community; to do so despite my lack of executive banking experience. To obtain all the necessary legal clearances and the required financing.

Writing out the problem is important because it helps you to understand exactly what it is, and it helps keep you on the track as you proceed to chart a solution. As you can see, Barry's problem was not just "starting a bank"—it was obtaining the knowledge, community support, and financing that would be required.

With those requirements in mind, Barry wrote the first four steps. Here, in abbreviated form, is what they looked like:

1. Bone up on state laws and practical procedures for getting a bank started; check library books and take a banking course at the community college.
2. Make a list of the town's businesspeople, then contact each of them about the idea of a local bank. Find out who would be interested in investing in such an institution.

3. Obtain a firm commitment and a small initial investment from each of the interested parties.

4. Use the initial funds to hire an attorney for guidance in forming a banking corporation.

Of course, there were many more steps involved in starting his bank, but you can see even from these abbreviated first four steps that a highly ambitious goal was suddenly made easier because of the one-step-at-a-time approach.

If you learn nothing else from this book than the statement you are about to read, you will have gained much:

> Nothing is so complicated that it can't be broken down into a series of simple, easy-to-understand and easy-to-accomplish steps.

As simple as this concept may appear to be, most people don't stop to realize that if a big problem is cut into enough little chunks, each of those chunks will be easy to resolve. Successfully completing Step 1 leads you naturally into Step 2, and before you know it, you're well down the list. That is how Barry got his bank established, and that is often how, to this day, he solves problems that crop up in his job as its chief executive officer.

HOW A FLOW CHART CAN HELP YOU

You may have wondered why, in talking about the process of writing out a step-by-step solution, I haven't called it a list instead of a chart. There's an important reason. A list goes from top to bottom, from Step 1 to Step 2, with no diversions along the way. A chart, on the other hand, can have entries to the left and right of the main steps.

Computer programmers have what they call a "flow chart." If the programmer knew from the outset just how everything would work out, he could merely list a set of step-by-step instructions, and it would indeed be a list instead of a chart. But often, in computer programming, the outcome of one step will determine what the next step is to be.

The computer in a membership organization may, for example, be programmed to see if John Smith renewed his membership. Then, depending on what it finds, the second step could be either of two alternatives.

STEP 1: Determine if John Smith's membership has been renewed.

If the answer is YES,
then perform STEP 2A.
If the answer is NO,
then perform Step 2B.

STEP 2A:	STEP 2B:
Send John Smith a membership card for the current year and see that his name remains on the membership roll.	Send John Smith a reminder, noting that his membership has expired and inviting him to send in his renewal promptly.

At the time the above steps were written, the computer specialist did not know what the outcome of Step 1 would be, and thus two alternatives were listed for Step 2. Similarly, when you begin to write out solutions to your problems, you may not know immediately what the outcome of certain steps will be. You, too, will be listing alternatives.

"That's another of the great benefits I get from charting solutions to my problems," reports self-made millionaire Keith T. "I am prepared for various eventualities, and I already have, on paper, alternative strategies for dealing with them."

Keith is a real estate operator whose projects include huge shopping centers, condominium projects, and resorts. As you might imagine, planning the projects and working out all of the arrangements involved can pose many problems. Keith deals with the major ones by committing them to paper, in chart form.

"First, I write down a sentence or two, stating what the problem is. Focusing my attention on the problem this way, I begin to see possible courses of action. I write these down in step-by-step form. When I encounter a step that would have unpredictable results, I write out the alternatives."

Like many problem solvers who use the charting method, Keith is familiar with this important principle:

The act of listing steps and charting alternatives serves as a mental lever, allowing you to concentrate all of your thought-resources on the one problem. This provides you with much more reasoning (problem-solving) power than would otherwise be possible.

"I find that after I begin to write out the problem, all kinds of helpful ideas come to me," Keith explains. "I write down every idea relating to the problem that I think of, even if it seems unworkable. Often, when you're thinking about something, you get a lot of 'stray' ideas about it that might not have much significance at the moment, but if you put them on paper, you've captured them permanently. Later, when you go over all of them, you combine some of these stray thoughts and arrive at remarkable solutions you never saw before."

HOW TO CHART AN EASY COURSE
FROM PROBLEM TO SOLUTION

There are only five basic steps in creating a chart that guides you from problem to solution:

1. Write a sentence or two explaining the problem.
2. Identify the desired outcome as clearly as you can.
3. Write all possible solutions that occur to you, whether or not they appear to be reasonable at the moment.
4. Study the possibilities you've listed and test them on paper. Take them from a logical first step right through to conclusion, listing each step along the way. When a particular step would have unpredictable results, list alternative actions to take next, as in the computer example you read earlier.
5. If the first set of steps leading from problem to solution does not please you, move on to one of the other possible solutions you have listed.

Although there's nothing magical about writing out a problem and the steps leading to its solution in this way, the results often seem magical. You'll see, when you actually try it, that the procedure gives a sharp new focus to your thinking, much more so than would otherwise be possible. The problem will be clarified as never before, and you'll discover solution possibilities that you hadn't known existed.

I have surveyed a number of people who use this method of dealing with tough problems, and each of them has given me some tips on how to make the system even more effective. Here are the tips that should help you the most:

* The business manager of a traveling rock band finds it best to stop halfway through the process of drawing up his solution chart. "I let the problem 'cook' while I go on to other things; then, when I get back to the chart, I have a fresh perspective," he says.

* A New York stockbroker uses his commuting time to work on problems. The hour he spends on the train each morning and evening is perfect for this. When problems crop up during the day, he makes a one-line note of them in his pocket diary, knowing that he'll have ample opportunity to chart them on the train. This frees up his working day for other productive chores.

* The random ideas that a Minneapolis sales executive writes down are what help her the most. "It's like running a one-person think tank," she reports. "One idea leads to another, and before I know it, there are dozens of exciting possibilities to consider."

* Occasionally I'm tempted to think it's silly," reports a California legislator, "to write out a problem I'm already familiar with, and the same with the desired outcome. But then, as I force myself to write down what I already know, I find myself struck with ideas I didn't know I could create. I mean workable ideas that present meaningful solutions, and I'm amazed that this simple process is able to bring them to the surface." Whenever he's tempted to skip the charting process, this lawmaker recalls what it's done for him in the past, and that's all the incentive he needs.

Try it just once with a problem that has been puzzling you, and I think you, too, will find it's all the incentive you need to make a lifetime habit of charting solutions. One thing is for sure: You'll consistently be solving problems that stump other people who aren't familiar with charting.

Combine charting with the other problem-solving weapons listed earlier in this chapter, and with the creative ideas outlined in Chapter 7, and you'll be equipped as never before to go out and beat the world.

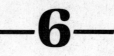

—6—

Instant Learning: How to Become a Wizard at Anything New

The world admires fast learners and rewards them well. Decision makers spot people who are able to pick up new subjects rapidly, and mark them for the most challenging and lucrative opportunities.

Here are two little-known facts about rapid learning:

1. Although rapid learning is often equated with a high IQ, Mental Leverage proves that the level of IQ is less important than how you use what you've got.

2. Unless you're lucky enough to have someone show you the way, it might take years of trial and error to acquire the rapid-learning techniques contained in this chapter.

With this book in your hands, you can count yourself as among the lucky. You're going to be shown the way by scores of people who have fine-tuned the most effective rapid-learning techniques. The methods they've developed enable anyone to pick up knowledge and skills in a fraction of the time normally required.

What are the most effective rapid-learning techniques? Here are some of the ones you'll discover in this chapter:

* Mental Activation
* Total Involvement

* Programmed Learning
* Personal Shorthand
* Enhanced Concentration

With these techniques in your pocket, you'll find learning new skills, taking on new jobs, and acquiring new talents a breeze. What's more, you won't be the only one to notice. Others won't be able to miss your mental quickness. In this chapter, you'll see real-life examples of how such recognition can bring you the lucrative opportunities that formerly passed you by.

MENTAL ACTIVATION: AN INSTANT-LEARNING TECHNIQUE

Athletes do it; so do chess players, executives, students, and people from all walks of life who seek to excel in their fields. What is it that they do? Whenever they're learning a subject that needs practice or repetition, they employ Mental Activation.

I'll explain what Mental Activation is by telling you about the members of a bowling team who had heard about Mental Activation and wondered if it could help improve their scores. They decided to give it a test by dividing the team members into three groups.

* Each member of Group A bowled for half an hour per day, for a period of twenty days. Their scores were taken on the first and last days of practice.

* Each member of Group B bowled on the first day when their scores were taken, and again on the twentieth day when their scores were again taken. On the second through the nineteenth days, they stayed away from the bowling lanes. On those days, however, they devoted the same amount of time (half an hour) to mental bowling. They pictured themselves doing the same type of practice as their colleagues in Group A, mentally going through all of the motions and experiencing each of the sensations.

* Each member of Group C bowled on the first and twentieth days, just as all of their colleagues did, but Group C did no practice of any kind (mental or physical) on the days in between. Their scores were taken on the first and twentieth days.

Here's the outcome:

* Group A, which undertook normal practice for the 20-day period, improved its scores by twenty-three percent.

* Group B, which practiced mentally for most of the days, improved its scores by twenty-two percent.

* Group C, which did not practice during most of the days, showed no improvement at all.

The team members discovered from this that, while practice is needed to improve their scores, it does not have to be physical practice. Mental practice, or Mental Activation, can be just as effective, provided you've had some physical practice to familiarize yourself with the correct procedures.

"What's the point," you may be wondering, "of using Mental Activation if it's only 'just as effective' as regular practice? Why not spend one's time doing the real thing?"

The point is that you can get in a lot more practice with Mental Activation because it can be done almost anywhere, such as when you are:

* Relaxing at home
* In a waiting room
* Walking or jogging
* Traveling by car, bus, train, or plane
* Eating a meal
* Listening to a dull speech
* Doing anything that does not require you to concentrate

People who employ Mental Activation can usually arrange to get in at least twice as much "practice" as their colleagues and competitors, which gives them a big advantage. But I sense that you have another question.

"Is Mental Activation only for developing physical skills?"

It has no such limitation. It can be a big boost to your mental learning as well. Alexander Alekhine was able to perfect his chess skills with Mental Activation by making moves in his mind and playing through entire games that way. Three months of such practice enabled him to beat the world champion and to eventually gain a reputation among his contemporaries as "the greatest chess genius of the 20th century."

Mental Activation is also used in learning foreign languages. By carrying on silent conversations with themselves, covering topics that are likely to come up in real conversation, foreign language students become much better prepared than if they only practiced in the classroom or with a book.

Mental Activation will, in fact, help you perfect your knowledge and skills in any field that:

1. has a set pattern of procedures, regardless of whether they are mental or physical

2. requires practice to make perfect

One of its great advantages is that it trains your mind to react automatically to conditions that might develop. A friend of mine who is a sailing buff uses Mental Activation to perfect her racing skills. She envisions various conditions that could occur during a sailboat race, and then she mentally goes through the motions of dealing with those conditions.

"I purposely make things tough on myself," Sharon says. "In fact, I win many more races in real life than I do in my mental practice!" The tough conditions she sets for herself during Mental Activation leave her fully prepared for the variations of wind and current that occur during actual sailing.

HOW TO USE MENTAL ACTIVATION

After you've done it a few times, you'll develop your own favorite ways of using Mental Activation, but here are some guidelines to get you started:

1. Do it only when you are refreshed and wide awake. (If you're not wide awake, the effect can be like counting sheep, and instead of getting valuable training, all you'll get is some slumber.) If you're a person who exer-

cises regularly, a good time to use Mental Activation is immediately after exercise sessions.

2. Do it at a time and in a place where distractions are unlikely.

3. Go through the entire procedure you want to perfect, from beginning to end. Picture yourself making every motion and experiencing every sensation involved in the procedure. Actually "feel" your muscles tense, if muscles are used in the procedure. You should really "feel" the emotions involved if the procedure is a mental one.

4. Always picture yourself performing flawlessly in whatever it is that you are practicing. If, for example, you are mentally shooting baskets on a basketball court, picture the ball going through the basket every time. This is important, because it gives you a positive self-image. Such confidence is vital to success in any field.

5. The length of your practice sessions should usually be between 15 and 30 minutes. Anything shorter than 15 minutes will probably not have a lasting effect, and anything longer than 30 minutes will be tiring and could erase the benefit of the positive self-image you are developing. It's perfectly o.k., however, to have several practice sessions per day.

A member of the bowling team you read about earlier practices several times per day, sometimes alternating actual physical practice with Mental Activation.

"I often go to the bowling lanes to practice for half an hour in the afternoon," Ray G. explains, "but the same day, as time allows, I'll probably also get involved in some 'mental' bowling as well. I've found this has the effect of multiplying the amount of practice I get in, since it seems to make no difference whether I bowl on the lanes or in my mind."

Psychologists don't have a complete answer as to why Mental Activation works so well, but they believe that creating a positive self-image has a lot to do with it. Doing something successfully over and over again—even if only in your mind's eye—gives you the confidence you need to continue doing it in real life.

The reflex training factor also has a lot to do with it. Mental Activation helps build your reflexes just the way regular training does. You prepare yourself for a variety of conditions that could develop and you know how to deal with them.

Ray G.'s Mental Activation is not confined to bowling. He also used it to help build a new career for himself. When the company Ray worked for moved to a distant city, Ray decided not to move with it. Instead, he took his life savings and opened a restaurant.

"I knew as much about the restaurant business as the average guy knows about Einstein's theory of relativity," Ray says, "but I figured I could learn. Mental Activation was a big help."

Although he considered himself a good amateur chef, Ray had never done it commercially before, and now he was going to have to turn out top quality dishes at a hectic pace.

"I knew the procedures involved," Ray recalls, "but when it comes to preparing complete meals on a volume basis—well, that was entirely new to me. Before opening the restaurant I went through a practice session in the kitchen and found that I was all thumbs. So I decided to augment that practice with Mental Activation.

"Whenever I had a spare quarter of an hour or so, I would sit down and mentally 'cook' half a dozen meals simultaneously, as you'd have to do in a restaurant. I envisioned each and every motion involved, and I built up my speed and confidence.

"On the day the restaurant opened for business, there was a good turnout of patrons, and I handled the kitchen chores with ease. I give Mental Activation a lot of credit for making my restaurant a success right from the start."

USE TOTAL INVOLVEMENT TO SPEED-LEARN ANY SUBJECT

"You can't learn how to swim until you get yourself wet."

That's the admonition I received while taking swimming lessons as a child at summer camp. Over the years, I've found that it goes not only for swimming, but for anything else that needs to be learned. You can receive all kinds of verbal instruction and read reams of theory, but you won't really learn the material until you get yourself totally involved in it.

"Total Involvement" in what you have learned, actually doing it rather than studying it, strongly reinforces your new knowledge and makes it much more meaningful. The rate of learning increases in direct proportion to the amount of Total Involvement you add to the standard "theoretical" learning. Thus if you are taking instruction along with a group of others, and you provide yourself with some Total Involvement as spelled out in this chapter, you'll learn faster and better than your colleagues.

At first glance, not all subjects seem to be of the "Total Involvement" type. It's easy enough to get involved in physical activities such as swimming or bowling, but what about math or psychology, or any of the new fields of knowledge you may need to learn in order to advance your career?

In such cases, Total Involvement may take a different form, but it still speeds the learning process by having you apply the information you have learned in a practical way. As you'll see, there are some powerful methods of applying any knowledge so that it becomes imbedded permanently in your mind, making you a much swifter learner than would otherwise be possible. Regardless of which method you use, here's what you should do:

1. Plan on using Total Involvement whenever you have read or been shown new material that you believe needs reinforcing in your mind.

2. Arrange to have the Total Involvement separated from the regular reading or instruction. In other words, when you read or are shown something new, give it time to be absorbed by your mind before you apply it in a Total Involvement session.

3. Better than one long practice session are two or more shorter sessions. This gives your mind a period of rest that, according to educators, allows your brain to sort out what it has learned and put it in proper perspective. The time between practice sessions can be as short as three or more minutes, or it can be a day or more.

THE TWO FORMS OF TOTAL INVOLVEMENT

While it might seem obvious that practical exercises help you learn a physical activity such as swimming, here's something that's not so obvious: providing yourself with practical exercises in nonphysical activities will benefit you just as much. Here are two examples:

* A businessman who was studying a foreign language to help in his dealings with overseas clients provided himself Total Involvement by (1) dining in ethnic restaurants where the language was spoken, (2) shopping in stores catering to people who spoke that language, and (3) listening to shortwave broadcasts. He particularly benefitted from Voice of America newscasts in the foreign language because they are usually delivered at a slow pace that is easier to understand.

* A keypunch operator who was studying computer programming at her local community college realized that she could benefit from some additional practical application of what she was learning. She bought an inexpensive home computer that worked through her television set. The practice she got with the home device speeded up her progress in the college course. She was the first person in her class to be hired as a programmer, and she now works for AT&T at twice her former pay as a keypuncher.

The first form of Total Involvement, then, has you putting your new knowledge to use in real-life situations. As you've seen, they can include swimming in a pool, ordering in a foreign restaurant, programming a computer, or gaining practical experience in whatever other field you're studying.

You're probably wondering what happens when it's not possible to use your knowledge in real-life situations. If, for example, you're studying for a real estate exam, it's impossible to "practice" the rules and regulations you've been learning. These are the occasions when you use the second form of Total Involvement.

You may be surprised at how simple the method is. Once

you start using it, you'll also be amazed at how effective it is. Here's the technique:

> Use your own words to write from memory what you learned in your most recent study or training session.

This written review should be done after some time has elapsed. Again, the purpose is to allow your brain to sift and sort the information. What makes this technique so effective? A very important principle:

> The act of recalling information and then writing it down has the same effect on mental training as field practice has on physical training.

In both cases, you are actively working with your newly acquired knowledge. You are forcing your memory to push the information to the most active part of your consciousness, and then you are using that information in the most practical manner possible. It's been proven that the best way to remember information is to put it to practical use soon after learning it. That's precisely what you're doing with Total Involvement.

Here are two examples of how colleagues of mine use the written review method to get totally involved in material they are learning:

* A direct-mail advertising executive who must attend frequent seminars and courses related to his work takes a few minutes in the evening following each session to summarize, in writing, the highlights of what he learned that day. "It's not the same as taking notes during class," he explains. "Class notes comprise a permanent record of what the instructor said. The object of writing a summary from memory is training, pure and simple. I put the information to practical use by expressing it in my own words. After doing this, the information stays with me a long, long time."

* An electronics engineer who must keep up-to-date on developments in that fast-moving field reads a lot of trade magazines and technical books. "First thing at my desk each morning," he says, "I take out a pad and pencil and write out a summary of the important information I learned the previous day. I find there's no

better way to reinforce the knowledge I've obtained and 'file' it away in a logical location in my brain."

Both of these men credit the written review method of Total Involvement with helping them progress rapidly in their complex fields. Each has gained a reputation as an expert with a superior array of knowledge. The simple, yet powerful, technique they use is available to anyone. Most people, however, are not aware of it—and, even if they were, they would probably be turned off by its simplicity, not recognizing its power to vastly improve their learning capacity.

But now you are aware of it. Give it a fair trial, and I'm sure that you, too, will reap great dividends from this fascinating Total Involvement technique.

HOW TO BENEFIT FROM PROGRAMMED LEARNING

Self-study courses, the kind that sell for hundreds of dollars, achieve much of their effectiveness because they use what is known as Programmed Learning. Often the only difference between a $15 textbook and a $350 self-study course is the manner in which the material is presented. All of the same information may be contained in the book and the course, but the course makes it a lot easier to read and learn.

Although it's probably not going to cost you one cent, Programmed Learning is worth all the extra money most people must pay for it. They'll pay the $335 difference between the price of a book and the cost of a course because Programmed Learning:

* Speeds up your learning and causes you to remember more
* Allows you to review the material without rereading long sections of text
* Is more enjoyable than regular studying
* Uses the highly effective question-and-answer method of making sure you fully understand the information

Instead of long, dull sessions spent reading a book, Programmed Learning consists of logical sections of information followed by easy review questions. Thus, you don't move on to new information until you've fully grasped what you've just read. Because it's almost like a game, the review process makes learning more fun, as well as more effective.

You're going to learn a simple means of devising your own Programmed Learning, and you'll get all the benefits of the expensive courses. It doesn't matter what your source material is. It can be:

* A textbook
* A magazine article
* A lecture
* A classroom demonstration
* Individual instruction

Regardless of the source of the information, it can be greatly enhanced by Programmed Learning (PL). PL is so powerfully effective because of these three factors:

1. Your memory of important information is increased when you employ more than one of your physical senses. Thus, in our form of PL, you review the material by using a physical sense other than the sense with which it was originally learned. If you studied the material by using your eyes (reading), then you'll use your ears (hearing) in the Programmed Learning review.
2. Because repetition of facts reinforces your memory of those facts, you'll be repeating the newly learned information in a unique way.
3. PL employs a process known as Active Recall, which causes you to actively think about the material. This implants it even further in your memory, but it has one other major advantage. It lets you know what information you have learned well, and what material needs further study.

Commercial courses that use PL usually have several paragraphs of text followed by a brief review section. The review section typically consists of a half-dozen sentences dealing with new material that was contained in the basic text. In the review section, however, the sentences are incomplete.

Blanks have replaced one or more of the key words, and it's up to you to fill in the blanks.

To illustrate, let's imagine that this is a PL course, and that the paragraph you have just read is followed by a PL review section. The review section might be set up like this:

1. In self-study courses, the PL format consists of several paragraphs of text followed by a brief _____ _____.
   (review section)

2. The sentences in the review section are _____.
   (incomplete)

3. One or more of the key words are replaced by _____ that you are to _____ _____.
   (blanks, fill in)

Using a sheet of paper to cover up the answers, the student reads each of the statements and attempts to fill in the blanks. It doesn't matter whether this is done mentally or in writing; the important part is that you make a concentrated effort to recall the material previously read. The incomplete sentences provide an easy format for that end.

IMPROVED QUALITY AND SPEED

The easy method you're about to learn for devising your own Programmed Learning was introduced to me by the executive director of a nationwide professional association. One of the purposes of the association is to keep its members up-to-date on the latest developments in their field, and thus it offers them a wide variety of books each year. The director realized that the members were having difficulty learning and remembering all that material, so he decided to share with them the Programmed Learning method he'd devised for himself.

He conducted seminars across the country to introduce the system to them, and they took to it eagerly. Over the years, hundreds of people have personally thanked him for showing them how to create their own Programmed Learning.

Many tell him they're able to learn twice as fast, giving them more free time for other activities. Equally important is the fact that the quality of their learning is improved along with the speed; in other words, they learn better as well as faster.

I was first shown the method at one of the seminars, and I've had occasion to use it a number of times. I'm as enthusiastic about this deceptively simple system as everyone else has been. I have been given permission to explain it here so that many more people can benefit from it.

HOW TO DEVISE YOUR OWN PROGRAMMED LEARNING

If the material you wish to learn is in text form, such as a book or magazine article, Programmed Learning is created with the aid of an inexpensive cassette recorder. Here's what you do:

1. As you read material that is new to you, stop whenever you encounter important points that should be remembered. Say that information into the recorder, but substitute the word "blank" for key words in the sentence. For example, you might record the following statement:

   "If the material you wish to learn is in text form, such as a book or magazine article, Programmed Learning is created with the aid of an inexpensive BLANK BLANK."

   Pause for two or three seconds, then state the words that should have gone wherever the word "blank" was spoken. (In the above example, the words would be "cassette recorder.") Stop the recorder, and turn it back on again when you come to the next important point that should be remembered. Repeat the procedure.

2. When you have recorded between five and ten such Programmed Learning sequences, or when you reach a logical "break" in the reading material such as the end of a chapter, rewind the cassette and play it back. With each sequence, stop the recorder at the point where there's a pause between the statement and the correct fill-in words. Try to recall the words. If you think you know them, compare your words with those that immediately follow the pause on the tape. If you were right, proceed to the next sequence. If you are not able

to recall the correct words, go back to the original reading material and give it another close look. Then proceed to the next sequence.

I am frequently asked why the person using this form of PL is allowed to look up the correct answers. The answer is that it's part of the learning process. The review section is not really a quiz, it's what its name implies; a review of what you've read. Your Active Recall of the missing words intensifies that review and makes it more effective. When you can't recall the correct words, you realize that you haven't learned the original material well enough, and so you go back over it.

A good idea is not to erase the review sections from the tape until you've completed the course of study that they deal with. At the end of the course, they can be played back again for a final review to help guarantee that you've retained all you need to know.

AN ALTERNATE FORM OF PL

You'll remember that one of the factors making PL so effective is that the review section employs a different physical sense. That's why a cassette recorder is used to review written material. But what about when you want to use PL with material that you've learned through verbal instruction, as in a classroom lecture? In this case, you reverse the process. If the material came to you through your ears, you review it with your eyes.

Instead of a tape recorder, you use a pencil and paper. At a convenient time after the class has ended, recall the important points (or go over any notes you might have taken) and write out, in PL format, the information you need to remember, inserting blanks in the place of occasional key words. You saw how this was done in the introduction to PL. Don't forget to list the key words in parentheses below each statement.

This procedure has a double impact. You are actually reviewing the material twice; first when you write out the key statements, and again when you read them over later and attempt to recall the words that belong in the blanks.

MAKING BETTER USE OF WHAT YOU LEARN

You may be wondering how taking extra time to prepare review statements can save you time in the long run. The answer lies in increased learning efficiency. Most people find that using the PL method causes them to learn and retain more information. Thus they perform better when using the information they've learned, making far fewer mistakes and getting the job done faster.

One of the first times I applied PL was shortly after I had bought a small computer system to help me in various word processing chores. I soon found, however, that the available word processing programs did not meet my needs. It became obvious that I'd have to write my own software, but never having written any before, it was just as obvious that I had a lot of learning to do.

Applying PL to my study of what is known in computer jargon as "assembly language programming," I was able to pick up the required skills rapidly, and wrote a complete word processing program that fully met my needs. Apparently I learned the subject especially well, because the program I wrote is used not only by me, but also by professionals and business people around the world who have bought it from me.

DOUBLE YOUR NOTE-TAKING SPEED

Taking notes can be a big help in learning something new, but most people are awkward and inefficient note-takers. They spend so much time writing out what they've heard, they often miss the next vital point being made by the speaker.

These two easily acquired skills can greatly increase your note-taking efficiency:

1. Personal shorthand
2. Mental editing

With just a few minutes' practice, you can develop these lifetime skills that will greatly increase your speed. I've used these two techniques for years, and they've not only been a big help to me, but they've also surprised other people. Often, when someone is feeding me information over the phone, I'm able to take it so rapidly that the other person becomes suspicious.

"Are you recording this on tape?"

I can't count the number of times I've been asked that question. And the answer has always been, "No, I take shorthand."

It's not real shorthand, at least not the type of shorthand stenographers take. It's a much easier type, one that is used by reporters, investigators, and all kinds of people who must take notes as part of their jobs. It involves a shorter way of writing words, and a mental editing process to determine which words you'll write.

Let's take a brief look at each skill and see how you can add it to your collection of Mental Leverage tools.

TOOL 1: PERSONAL SHORTHAND

The Personal Shorthand used by the great majority of news reporters, lawyers, investigators, and others who need quick writing skills does not resemble what professional sten-ographers use. Personal Shorthand uses real letters and regular handwriting. The only difference is that it uses fewer letters in each word.

The method: drop most vowels. As an example, consider this phrase:

Drop most vowels.

Instead of writing it out as you see it printed above, write it out this way:

Drp mst vwls.

With just this simple change, you have eliminated more than twenty-five percent of the writing. The original phrase had fourteen letters; the modified form has ten. Here's another example:

The real benefit of this technique is that it maintains full readability with far fewer letters.

The sentence, written in the kind of Personal Shorthand that I use, would look like this:

T rl bnft of ths tknk is tht it mntns fl rdblty w/fr fwr ltrs.

By the way, in saying it maintains full readability, I mean for you, the person who wrote it. Another person would probably have difficulty deciphering what you wrote down in Personal Shorthand. But since you wrote the information that you heard, the abbreviated words will have full meaning to you. Also, the context helps you. Consider the second word in the example above: "rl" could mean any number of words such as role, rail, or rule, but you know from the context of the sentence that it stands for real.

Everyone develops his own Personal Shorthand "tricks," and you can see several of mine above. You can see that:

1. I use the letter "T" standing alone to designate the word "the."
2. Some short words such as "of" and "is" are written out for clarity.
3. Double consonants such as the l's in "full" need be written only once.

These are not rules for you to memorize. In fact, the only rule in Personal Shorthand is that you should drop most vowels. With just a bit of practice, you'll develop your own technique and habits that make it truly a personal form of shorthand. I can, however, let you in on some of the variations developed by people I know. Just as no one person has adopted all of these techniques, all of them won't be for you. But here are some things to consider:

* Don't cross T's. If the upstroke is high enough, it will be recognizable to you as a T.
* Don't dot lower-case i's. The upstroke won't be as high as a T, and thus the letter will be distinguishable.
* Develop your own abbreviation for words you use frequently, particularly words in your trade or profession. (A lawyer I know writes a capital C every time he means court, D for defendant, P for plaintiff, etc.)

* When letters have a lower loop (such as in y and j), eliminate the loop by writing a single downstroke.
* Use symbols for common words such as "and" and "with."

One final tip: In writing out your abbreviated words, use letters that indicate the way they sound, not the way they are normally spelled. Here's a sentence written in everyday English, followed by the way it might appear in Personal Shorthand:

Everyday English:

I had a rough time getting him to come to the phone quickly.

Personal Shorthand:

I hd a rf tm gtng hm to km to t fn kwkly.

You can see that the "gh" in "rough" and the "ph" in phone have been converted to "f," and the hard "c" in "come" has been changed to a "k," as has the "q" in "quickly."

The best way to start using PS is to transcribe written material. Take a few sentences from a newspaper, magazine, or this book, and write them in your note pad in PS form. Don't take PS notes of the spoken word until you (1) develop some speed and (2) have become familiar with Mental Editing, a technique that will enable you to keep up with even the fastest speaker.

TOOL 2: MENTAL EDITING

The important thing to remember, when you are taking notes in Personal Shorthand, is that you are not a stenographer who must write down every word that is spoken. In fact, in most cases you don't even have to write down all of the main points. Just write (in abbreviated PS format) the specific information you wish to remember. This will probably require far fewer words than those used by the speaker.

Even people who make their living dispensing information every day use far too many words. With a little practice, you can make instant decisions as to what to write down and what to bypass, and you'll probably find that nine-tenths of what you hear goes the bypass route.

When professional people dole out information, they generally do it in three phases:

1. They tell you the nature and importance of the information they are about to dispense,
2. They dispense the actual information, and
3. They remind you of the nature and importance of the information they have just dispensed.

In other words, they tell you what they're going to tell you, they tell it to you, and then they tell you what they've told you. A stenographer would have to write down every word that is spoken, but all you need is the middle part. Don't waste your time on the introduction and review.

You may never have noticed before how much repetition occurs when people are dispensing information. Much of it serves to amplify or explain the main point. But when you are taking notes for the purpose of learning a new subject, you can skip the extra material, writing down just the main points. Later, when you review these main points, you'll be automatically reminded of the related material that was given by the speaker.

How much practice does it take to develop the knack of Mental Editing? Very little. Listen closely the next time you hear someone giving a lengthy explanation on TV. Consider what you would actually have to write down if you were taking notes on that subject. You'll find it's one-third or less of what the speaker actually says.

Let's do some calculating. With Mental Editing, you need write down less than one-third of what is said. And, thanks to Personal Shorthand, the writing process itself is shortened by twenty-five percent. The introduction to this section said you could double your note-taking speed. As you can see, you'll probably do much better than that.

HOW TO INCREASE YOUR POWER OF CONCENTRATION

Watch an expert at work and you'll discover that one of the secrets of his success is concentration. Try to distract him from what he is doing and either you'll find it very difficult to do so, or you'll find that the expert is angry with you for having made the attempt. He knows that concentration is vital to his success.

People who practice Mental Leverage know the rules for effective concentration. They get the most mileage out of their learning periods by setting up the right conditions for themselves. These conditions provide the key to effective concentration.

The first condition is desire. It's virtually impossible to concentrate unless you are vitally interested in the subject. What if you're not vitally interested? You can become so by considering your goal—the reason you are studying the subject. Whenever you feel "down" about studying, ask yourself two questions:

1. How will I benefit by learning this?
2. What will I lose out on if I don't learn this?

Visualizing the goal and benefits will spark your interest as well as your ability to concentrate.

The second condition is being wide awake so that you can absorb the new material easier. One trick is to keep the room cool—sixty-five degrees Fahrenheit or under. Performers know this trick well, and they use it to keep their audiences alert. You've already experienced what the opposite does. How many times have you been made drowsy by an overly warm room? Studying on a full stomach will also put you to sleep, so never begin soon after a meal.

The third condition is taking advantage of your "day person" or "night person" status. Experience has shown you whether you function best in the morning or at night. Virtually everyone falls into one category or the other. Use your best period of the day to study, and you'll learn more efficiently.

And the fourth condition is to follow the study with a period of relatively light mental activity. Tests have shown that newly learned material can be lost if the person quickly turns to other activities requiring concentrated thought. Thus, if you're a night person, arrange your studying for just before you go to bed. A day person might study just before showering and leaving for work: activities that won't provide the type of mental interference that is to be avoided.

Set up these four conditions for yourself, and your ability to concentrate will improve significantly. You'll discover why effective concentration is one of the most powerful tools there is for becoming a wizard at anything new.

Unlocking the Creative Genius of Your Mind

Creativity isn't just for artists. It's a big boost to success in any field. People who know how to come up regularly with ingenious ideas and solutions are the ones who advance fastest in their careers, build more profitable businesses, attract the smartest people as their friends and associates, and live the most problem-free lives.

Creativity is a quality all of us possess. Unfortunately, most people haven't learned how to make regular use of it. For a variety of reasons, they keep the bulk of their creative genius locked up in the recesses of their minds, unavailable for everyday use. This chapter reveals how to unlock it and thus release your full potential as a creative problem solver and achiever.

INGENUITY: HOW TO MAKE IT PAY OFF

"Gee, how'd he ever think of that?"

Isn't that what you've often wondered when someone has arrived at a highly unusual solution to a problem? When problems don't appear to be solvable in the usual way, creative people don't hesitate to think of entirely new approaches.

Take Ulysses S. Grant as an example. Abraham Lincoln liked to tell about the time when Grant, as a boy, used ingenuity to defeat a stubborn mule that would not let anyone ride it. The mule was so intractable that it was bought by a circus operator, who offered money to anyone who could ride it for a prescribed period of time.

Grant saw several grown men try, only to be thrown off. He gave it a go and managed to stay on for almost the full length of time, but then he, too, was thrown. Finally, the youngster called upon his ingenuity. Obtaining permission to make another attempt, he attacked the problem from a different angle.

Rather than climb on in the usual way, he boarded the mule backwards, facing the tail instead of the head. The boy coiled his legs around the animal's stomach and grabbed the tail with both hands. Try as it could, shaking and bucking, the mule could not throw him. The stubborn mule was defeated, and Ulysses S. Grant won the prize.

Soon after Grant had grown up and won the Civil War, James Ritty, another American, was aboard a steamship bound for Europe and took note of a piece of equipment that counted the revolutions of the ship's propeller. The recording device provided the navigator with a periodic report of the boat's speed.

Ritty envisioned a similar type of record-keeping device for merchants: one that, instead of noting propeller revolutions, would keep a record of cash sales and total them up at the end of the day. This led him to invent the cash register.

The experiences of Grant and Ritty illustrate the two major uses of ingenuity:

1. Finding unusual solutions to tough problems (as Grant did in riding the ass backwards), and

2. Giving birth to new concepts (as Ritty did with the cash register).

Mental Leverage makes it possible for anyone to excel at both kinds of ingenuity. But before I show you how, there are two requirements we must discuss.

EQUIP YOURSELF FOR INGENUITY

Zacharias said, "Man is the favorite of nature, not in the sense that nature has done everything for him, but that she has given him the power of doing everything for himself." The trouble is, we don't recognize this power. The great majority of us lack the confidence to try anything even slightly unusual.

Confidence is one of the prime ingredients of ingenuity. When you know there is a way to solve a problem (even though you may not yet know what that way is) you have the incentive to dig for the solution. People who come up with one ingenious idea after another are really no more creative than the rest of us. They simply have more confidence.

How can you build that same kind of confidence? By knowing what they know:

> There is a solution to every problem and an idea to meet every need.

Experience will bear this statement out. In this chapter, you'll learn how to start using your ingenuity in situations you never would have attempted before. You'll demonstrate to yourself that there is indeed a solution to every problem and an idea to meet every need. You'll also discover how easy it is to find them.

Confidence, then, is the first requirement of ingenuity. You may be surprised to learn that the second is independence. Alexander Graham Bell said:

> Don't keep forever on the public road, going only where others have gone. Leave the beaten path occasionally and dive into the woods. You will be certain to find something you have never seen before. One discovery will lead to another, and before you know it, you will have something worth thinking about. All really big discoveries are the result of thought.

The independent thinker is not bound by the prescribed way of doing things. He isn't floored just because the rules say something can't be done in a certain way. Regardless of what the "experts" may say, he knows there is a solution to every problem and an idea to meet every need, and he's not afraid to consider unusual possibilities.

No one else thought of mounting the animal backwards but, by considering that unusual possibility, Ulysses S. Grant won the contest. More examples of independent thinking follow:

* Normal police tactics were proving unsuccessful in dealing with a burglary ring that specialized in clothing stores. In one break-in after another, the thieves moved in and stripped the racks so rapidly that they were gone by the time the police arrived. Burglar alarms and other sophisticated devices were of no help. Then, an independent-thinking detective advised the merchants to alternate their hanger hooks, turning one toward the wall and the next toward the center of the room, all along the rack. Having to remove the clothing item-by-item slowed the thieves down so much that, the next time a burglar alarm went off, the officers arrived at the store while the burglars were still trying to gather their loot.

* A man's lifelong dream to start a local radio station seemed thwarted by a group of businessmen who filed with the FCC to obtain a broadcasting license to serve the same county. Not only that but, a few months later, another company filed a competing application for the same area and the same spot on the radio dial. The hopeful station owner's ingenuity came to the rescue. "Why fight it out in a three-way race?" he thought. "Why not eliminate the competition?" After some study, he found a different frequency on the dial—and a better one at that. It made it possible to broadcast a non-directional signal that could be heard throughout the entire county, while the firm that won the original frequency would have a directional signal not heard in many local communities. The upshot: the man who found a better frequency got on the air, while the businessmen were still fighting it out. His station became a quick success. The other station, when it finally won its license, was a failure and lasted for only a few years.

If you'll recognize the fact that there is a solution to every problem and an idea to meet every need, and if you're willing to be an independent thinker who is unafraid to leave the beaten path occasionally, you'll come up with ingenious solutions whenever you need them.

PROBLEM-SOLVING WITH INGENUITY

Here's a way to activate your ingenuity in solving the toughest problems you'll ever have to face. Begin by learning this fact:

When a problem can't be solved in the conventional way, it's usually because of a missing link.

Grant's problem of not being able to stay on the mule the first time was in the lack of something to hold onto. That was the missing link. The police department's missing link in the clothing store burglaries was the lack of sufficient time from when the burglar alarm sounded to when the thieves fled with their loot.

Thus, the first step in seeking an ingenious solution to a tough problem is to determine the nature of the missing link. Your objective is to find the one element that, if it were provided, would solve the problem. Don't worry at first about whether or not it's possible to provide that element (or link). Just think about identifying it.

The missing link will sometimes be obvious (as in Grant's lack of something to hold onto), but on other occasions it will take some digging. That's fine, because it starts your creative juices flowing, in directions you might never have thought of otherwise.

When the man who dreamed of starting a local radio station asked himself about the missing link, he had to dig for an answer. With three parties competing for the same radio frequency, it may not seem as if there was such a thing as a missing link, just too much competition. But thinking about it for a while provided this answer: the missing link was a spot on the dial for which there was no competition.

HOW TO USE THE MISSING LINK TECHNIQUE

Here, then, are the two steps for using the Missing Link Technique in finding ingenious solutions to tough problems:

1. Identify the missing link between the problem and its solution. What is the one element that would, if it were available, eliminate the problem? At this point, don't be specific; think of it in general terms. (Before Grant could dream up the idea of grabbing the tail, he had to realize that the missing link was something to hold onto.)

2. This is where a willingness to be independent comes in. Regardless of how crazy they may seem at first, consider all the possibilities you can think of for filling in the missing link. You might want to write them down as they occur to you. Don't be too quick to eliminate any of the possibilities. Instead, consider the various ways they might be implemented. You'll arrive at solutions you never would have thought of otherwise, and then you can choose the one that offers the most advantages.

Back in the 1930s, Aramco, the Arabian-American Oil Company, needed vehicles that could be driven on the Saudi Arabian desert. The problem was the sand; there was a lack of traction, and wheels often dug in. Time is money, even to oil companies, and every time the wheels spun, time and money were lost.

There having been no prior research on the subject, Aramco engineer Richard Kerr didn't have engineering data to use in designing tires that would provide the precise traction needed on the desert sand. Thus, Step One of the Missing Link Technique was identifying the missing link as the lack of engineering data.

Step Two was to consider all of the possibilities for obtaining suitable data. Trial and error was one possibility, but that would take too much time. As he allowed his mind to roam freely toward all possibilities, one of the engineer's ideas was to imitate camels, which have no trouble at all moving across the desert. Despite their bulk and weight, camels don't get stuck in the sand.

Crazy as the camel possibility might seem at first, it stood to reason that the kind of traction that worked for them would work for motor vehicles as well. He measured the spread of their feet and took their weight. This provided him with the "engineering data" to determine the shape and pressure of the tires needed on the desert.

The solution he devised is still in use today—and not just in the Middle East. The tires you see on dune buggies are the grandchildren of the ones the Aramco engineer designed.

The Missing Link Technique is an important ingredient of your Mental Leverage tool chest. Don't let its simplicity deceive you. It's a surprisingly effective device for getting the most out of your natural ingenuity. It establishes highly creative thinking patterns that enable you to dream up innovative solutions to all kinds of problems.

Try it the next time you're stumped. First, determine the missing link between the problem and its solution. Then start counting off the various possibilities for providing that link. As Alexander Graham Bell said, you will be certain to find something you have never seen before.

HOW TO COME UP WITH INGENIOUS NEW IDEAS

So far, we've been talking about using ingenuity to solve problems. How about using it to create ideas that, rather than solving problems, offer exciting new opportunities?

Many of the world's most useful discoveries were, as I'm sure you know, made accidentally. Isaac Newton got hit on the head by an apple, the story goes, and this led him to discover the law of gravity. Many inventors didn't set out to invent their most notable products; they were working on other projects when an incident along the way caused them to change course and come up with something far different from and much more important than what they had imagined.

William H. Mason, for example, was trying to find a way to extract turpentine from green lumber. In visiting many sawmills, he noticed the great amount of wood going to waste. He dropped his turpentine project and began to think of ways to combine those small pieces of scrap lumber into usable material. Thus was born his idea of reducing the wood to fibers and then pressing them into hard panels, resulting in the familiar Masonite.

It's entirely natural for discoveries and inventions to be created this way; one idea leads to another, and the original idea is dropped while the newest one develops into a much more significant project than had been envisioned.

And this brings us to the point. New ideas are never entirely original. They are combinations or adaptations of other ideas. James Ritty invented the cash register based on what he saw the navigators using aboard ship. Richard Kerr developed tires for the desert based on the natural equipment camels are born with. Even U.S. Grant's idea for riding the mule wasn't entirely original. Wasn't it similar to grabbing the reins while riding a horse?

The engineers and scientists who staff a large European research center are greeted, as they report to work each day, by a plaque in the center's entrance hall. It contains this three-sentence quotation attributed to Dr. George Grier:

> It is not at all likely that anyone ever had a totally original idea. He may put together old ideas into a new combination, but the elements which made up the new combination were mostly acquired from other people. Without many borrowed ideas there would be no inventions, new movements or anything else that is classed as new.

Oliver Wendell Holmes put it another way, saying, "Many ideas grow better when transplanted into another mind than in the one where they sprang up." So why struggle and sweat to create new ideas, when the very idea you need already exists in a somewhat different form? Just think of the possibilities! No longer will you need to depend on "inspiration" to come up with creative thoughts; instead, you can take tried and proven ideas, combining or adapting them so they fit your needs.

WHY YOU SHOULD BE A CREATIVE COPYCAT

Most of the people in business, science, and the arts who consistently come up with the brightest ideas are really what I call Creative Copycats. They take proven products, formulas, and systems and adapt them to their own use.

A perfect example of this is a young novelist who recognized the tremendous odds against writing a best-selling book. More than 40,000 books are published each year, and only a relative handful make it to the Top Ten Best-Seller List. This particular writer spent six months reading 100 past best-sellers to learn what they had that he needed. His search paid off handsomely, for Robin Cook then wrote "Coma," which promptly made it to the best-seller lists and became the first of a string of highly successful books for him.

As I point out in my own best-selling business book, *How Self-Made Millionaires Build Their Fortunes,* too many people spend a lifetime waiting for "the big idea" to hit them when all the while big ideas surround them, ready to be tapped. A big idea is staring you in the face every time you:

* Walk into a store
* Read an ad
* Use a product
* Sign a check
* Pass a billboard
* Read a newspaper
* Watch a machine operate

Do you know how King Gillette got the idea for the safety razor with throwaway blades? No, he did not start out with the thought that the world needed a better razor. He got his idea from the cork that was then used inside the caps of soft drink bottles. He spotted this cork as a nearly perfect commercial product—a disposable item that the customer must obtain over and over again.

Gillette thought of various ways of adapting this idea to other uses, and he settled on the razor. Up until then, permanent blades continually needed stropping to remain sharp and occasionally had to be taken to a cutler for professional sharpening. He realized that inexpensive throwaway blades would be a great convenience to the customer, and a never-ending source of profit for him.

The idea for printing was not drawn out of thin air. It was suggested by initials that had been carved into a tree. A boy's curiosity about the optical effects created by two pieces of glass led to the invention of the telescope.

The success of McDonald's hamburger restaurants has

sparked many imitations. As you know, there are a number of other hamburger chains using the same fast-service principle. But Creative Copycats have also adapted that principle for use in other fields.

For example, instant hamburgers led to instant printing. Having only a few items on the menu, each restaurant can produce them quickly and inexpensively. The thousands of quick-print shops also limit their "menus" to a few, limited types of printing while you wait, and do it cheaply.

In the same vein, drive-in banks led to drive-up photo kiosks in shopping centers; self-service laundries sparked the idea for self-service car washes, and the success of book clubs has led to record clubs.

CURIOSITY: YOUR MOST VALUABLE CREATIVE ASSET

The right hemisphere of the brain is where we think our creative thoughts. Children are able to access the right hemisphere much easier than most adults can, and that's why kids always seem to have the most creative ideas. Their imaginations are not held back by the left hemisphere of the brain, which is where logic is stored.

The closer to adulthood one gets, the more dominant the left hemisphere of the brain becomes. As soon as something creative pops up on the right side of the brain, the left side warns that it doesn't make sense, it can't be done, it's against the rules, or it'll make people laugh at us.

Fortunately, not every adult has lost the ability to make good use of the right hemisphere of the brain. These people have been able to hold onto the childlike quality of curiosity. It is said that curiosity killed the cat, but curiosity is the lifeblood of Creative Copycats.

And, yes, some adults who lost that quality have been able to regain it. They've done it by applying the same elements of Mental Leverage that you are about to learn. The right side of your brain is no smaller than it used to be, and Mental Leverage proves that it's really no weaker. All you need do is reprogram yourself to use it.

HOW TO PROGRAM YOURSELF FOR CREATIVITY

Here's a five-step program that will reopen the channels of communication to the creative side of your mind. Incorporate these steps into your daily living pattern, and you'll soon find yourself coming up with innovative ideas you never would have thought of before. Such ideas can be a big boost to your career, your business, and to your success in pursuing spare-time interests.

Here are examples with each of the steps to get you started.

1. Experiment with different ways of doing many of the things you do. The point is not necessarily to find better ways, but to rebuild your mental flexibility, which is your willingness and ability to keep looking at things from different angles.

   EXAMPLES: Try a different method or route of commuting to work; occasionally attend a different church (even if it's the same denomination); change the physical format of your business letters or memos; develop different strategies for your golf, tennis, or chess games; in restaurants, order foods you've never tried before.

2. Give new ideas a chance to survive. Most people scoff at half-baked ideas, not realizing that *all* ideas are half-baked at first. With a little polishing, even the looniest-appearing idea may turn out to be a gem. Don't be any quicker to reject someone else's "farfetched" ideas than you are with your own. In either case, the imaginative effort needed to study and develop the idea is great for you, and even if the plan ultimately has to be dropped, the mental calisthenics still did you a lot of good.

   EXAMPLE: We're all struck with new ideas for doing things many times each day. We lose them just as quickly. Either a distraction causes us to think of something else, or the left hemisphere of our brain tells us the idea is no good. Two things to do: carry a notebook or a pocket recorder with you, and make a permanent record of such ideas right after they've struck you. Later, give yourself an opportunity to think them through.

3. Develop your ability to be a Creative Copycat. As we've noted, all new ideas are really combinations or adaptations of existing ideas. There's a way you can condition your mind to come up with these combinations and adaptations. It takes a little practice, but it's fun and it'll pay big dividends. Spend ten minutes each day thinking how two unrelated products, systems, or situations are similar. List all of the similarities you can think of. The next day, go on to two other unrelated items. This, in itself, is not likely to generate any brilliant ideas for you, but here's what it will do: it will get your mind thinking about relationships and similarities, even when you're not playing this little game. That's how your best ideas will be produced.

EXAMPLE: A car and a television set don't appear to be similar at all. But here are just a few of the similarities you might think of: both are made on assembly lines; in both cases, Japanese imports have severely cut into American production; they share many similar components such as electrical wiring, knobs, antennas, dials, and switches; they are the two most common "expensive" possessions of American families; giant repair industries have been built to service each product.

4. Develop some creative pastimes. They help keep your imagination fit and ready for action. Creativity should not be an all-work-and-no-pleasure sort of thing. It fits into every part of your life, and if you can find enjoyable ways to keep it strong, all the better. Just as the muscles you develop in a gym will help you pick up boxes, the "creative" muscles you develop in creative pastimes will help in your career.

EXAMPLES: Work on puzzles, play competitive board games, paint, write, learn photography and craftwork, and get involved in community theater activities. One person I know gets a big creative boost out of repairing appliances for friends because when parts are broken or missing, he has to do so much improvising.

5. Be inquisitive. Never be satisfied with mere facts; seek to learn reasons as well. Develop the habit of asking questions—of yourself as well as others—even when the topic is not immediately important to you. It's not the knowledge you'll gain that counts, but rather the strengthening of your curiosity. The curiosity of most adults has withered. Isn't it time you rebuilt yours?

EXAMPLES: The next time you finish reading a newspaper, ask yourself why you read certain items and skipped others. Ask your friendly grocer why he picked that particular location for his store. Ask the next candidate who solicits your vote why he favors his political party over the others. The next time somebody tells you something can't be done, ask why not. If his answer doesn't settle it, ask him about that as well. Whenever you have something repaired, ask what went wrong and why.

THE BACKWARD CHALLENGE

A frequently effective way to spur creativity is to discover a solution and then go out looking for a problem to fit that solution. Confused? Read on.

As you've seen many times in this chapter, creativity comes from looking at things from a different angle. For example, you may be a production manager who is stuck with a warehouse full of made-to-order plastic pipe because the construction company that ordered it declared bankruptcy. The special lengths and sizes make the pipe hard to sell to another construction outfit, and you need the space. This, obviously, is a problem. But it might also be a solution to one of your other problems.

Dealing in pipe makes your company heavily dependent on construction cycles; when buildings aren't being constructed, your sales drop off. Perhaps you can find new uses for this odd-sized pipe—uses not related to the construction industry. Through that, maybe you can develop an entirely new market.

This is not a hypothetical case. It happened, and the production manager who was faced with the problem is now an

executive vice-president. That's because he proposed that his
company sell the plastic pipe to a patio furniture manufacturing company, one that specializes in plastic furniture with
frames that appear to be made of pipe. Offered a discount
price, the manufacturer bought the warehouse full of pipe, and
this led to a steady business relationship between the two
companies.

Sooner or later, someone else in the pipe company would
probably have had the same idea, but the production manager
was first, so he's the one who was rewarded for being innovative.

The rewards for innovation can be yours, too, if you make
a habit of examining unusual or unexpected situations as possible opportunities. Make productive use of all that curiosity
that's being revived within you; ask yourself if each such situation isn't really a solution just waiting for a problem. If
nothing else, you'll come up with a lot of ideas and possibilities
before anyone else does. That's what being creative is all about.

YOUR SUBCONSCIOUS: A STREAM OF IDEAS AND SOLUTIONS

Several times, in this chapter, I have pointed out that
there is a solution to every problem and an idea to meet every
need. Now I'm going to expand on that just a bit. The odds are
great that the makings of those solutions and ideas are already
stored in your mind.

There are figures to back me up. Scientists estimate that
during the typical lifetime, close to fifteen trillion bits of data
are sent to the human brain. Everything you have ever experienced is recorded there. If trillions of bits of data exist there,
just think of how many zillions of different combinations could
be formed from them! With all that potential, there is bound to
be the answer you need.

That's the good news. The bad news is that ninety percent of that information is buried in your subconscious, and
there's no simple way to "will" it out into the open. It comes out
as it wants to, not the way you consciously wish it would. You
can't force out a specific hunch or creative idea. You can't order
your subconscious to release the precise data you need, this
instant. It doesn't work that way. It needs some time for sifting

and rearranging. Then, when perhaps you least expect it, the answer will come.

Here's how and why it works:

* When you have been consciously striving to create an idea or arrive at a solution, your subconscious is also aware of what you are seeking.

* Your subconscious never rests, even when you're asleep. It is constantly sorting and sifting the trillions of bits of data that it holds.

* Minutes, hours, or even days after you have stopped mulling over a particular problem, your subconscious will flash a solution to you. You are suddenly struck by an idea, or the answer to a tough problem comes to you while you're thinking of something else.

The person who first used the expression, "sleep on it" was wise indeed. More important ideas and discoveries have been made during or following a period of sleep than you can shake a pillow at. I'm sure you realize they all came from the subconscious.

Sir Walter Scott certainly knew that. He never let problems bother him. He knew that most times he would have the answer upon arising in the morning. Einstein felt the same way, reporting that he got his best ideas while shaving. Thomas Edison would—after a period of trying to solve a tough problem and failing—decide to abandon it for twenty-four hours. At some point during that twenty-four hour period, undoubtedly after a period of sleep, the answer would come to him. Mozart told friends that some of his best work was composed while he was dozing. Upon awakening, he would write down the score of the music he had "heard" in his slumber.

Lest you misunderstand, one thing needs emphasizing: each of these people was already an expert in his field. He did not develop his genius from ideas that came to him during sleep. The subconscious can only sort out information that you have already acquired over the years and "report" that information to you as needed.

That's why creative people depend on their subconscious not as a crutch, but as a tool to help them make the most of the knowledge and creativity they know is already stored in their minds. Those who benefit the most are the ones who are familiar with the workings of the subconscious (as you now are) and have learned, through experience, that they can depend on it.

The usual procedure, as you've seen, is to prime your subconscious by reviewing the appropriate facts and considering possible solutions. Then, if suitable ideas are still lacking, the matter is laid to rest with the knowledge that the desired information will come. At some point—probably while your mind is at relative ease—the answer should strike you, seemingly "out of the blue."

In case you're wondering: yes, it is possible to speed things up a bit. You can consciously take up the problem again after it has had time to incubate. Try this the next time you're stumped: lay the problem down for an hour or two. Go on to other things, preferably activities that don't require heavy mental work. Then go back to your problem. You'll discover ideas and possibilities that completely escaped you the first time.

Although you had let the matter "rest" for a while, your subconscious continued to work on it. You'll find that you can feed all kinds of problems to your subconscious and receive back a steady flow of creative ideas that, without the techniques you've learned here, might have remained forever buried.

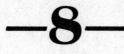

Wildcatting
for Ideas
and Solutions

Wildcatters, as you probably know, are people who drill oil wells in territory not known to be oil fields. They keep drilling until they either find oil or run out of money. The odds are against them, but the reward if they do strike oil can be fabulous.

This chapter is about another kind of wildcatting which, instead of oil, drills for ideas and solutions. Unlike the oil variety, it costs nothing (except a few minutes of your time) and the odds are exceedingly good. People who use Mental Wildcatting can almost always come up with whatever idea or solution they are seeking.

Look at it this way: if an oil wildcatter were able to drill enough holes in enough different locations, sooner or later he would strike a gusher. The same with Mental Wildcatting, except that since you're drilling for ideas instead of black gold, you know a lot more about where to search. Your "gusher" comes in much faster and at no financial cost to you.

WILDCATTING: A POWERFUL FORM OF MENTAL LEVERAGE

You've learned many different ways to apply Mental Leverage, and some of the best ways are still to come. Wildcatting

133

is one of them because it works so easily and well. It's also a lot of fun.

As you've seen in previous chapters, Mental Leverage makes a little bit of mental effort accomplish what normally would require a lot of mental effort. Wildcatting fits precisely into this mold, because it enables people to quickly obtain ideas and solutions that might otherwise take long days or even weeks of mental struggle.

How does Mental Wildcatting work? It begins with this: when seeking an idea or solution, you take paper and pencil and write down every possibility that occurs to you. You write it instantly, without stopping to decide whether or not it is feasible, just as the oil wildcatter drills in unknown territory. "Far out" ideas are not only acceptable, they are encouraged. You write as many ideas as you can, and then set the paper aside. Later you take another piece of paper and perform a somewhat similar procedure, bringing additional ideas to the surface. Depending on the circumstances, you might even write down the ideas of your colleagues as well.

Then comes the evaluation session, and it will bring some surprises. Using a special technique to score the dozens (perhaps hundreds) of items on your list, you discover that about six percent of them are practical, and that one or two may be absolutely brilliant.

Most people who use Wildcatting find that, compared to their former methods of searching for ideas and solutions, it gives them answers that are:

* Totally unexpected
* Resourceful
* Far superior

People use Wildcatting when they need highly original ideas and when they need down-to-earth, everyday solutions. Here's how some of the people I know profit from it:

* A television programming executive depends on Wildcatting to help him come up with ideas for new shows each year.

* The regional manager for a fast-food chain periodically closes the door to his office, tells his secretary to hold

all calls, and uses the Wildcat process to solve his most stubborn problems.

* An account executive for a large advertising agency generates ideas for new ad campaigns by Wildcatting.

* A housewife who was elected to her local school board uses Wildcatting to lay plans for dealing with the annual budget squeeze.

* A trial lawyer prepares for tough cases by Wildcatting for strategy that will win in court.

RELEASING THE RAM CELLS OF YOUR MIND

RAM is a computer term that stands for random access memory. It's the section of a computer that stores data for later retrieval. For example, as I write this book using a word-processing computer, each of the words is stored in random access memory. Should I wish to change a word or sentence, the material can be recalled from RAM, altered, and then sent back to RAM.

> **ran'dom ac'cess,** adj: 1. allowing access to stored data in any order the user wishes; 2. equal access to any desired memory location in a computer.

The human mind and the computer have often been likened to one another, and while I won't get into the argument about whether or not computers can think, I will point out that they both store much of their data in random access memories, meaning the "user" can access any part of the information and in any order he chooses.

That, in fact, is what you do when you Wildcat. You pick a subject that needs ideas or solutions, and then you access the sections of your mind that hold thoughts, memories, flashes of information, beliefs, and any other "data" that is pertinent to the subject. Out comes a steady stream of suggestions that you write down for safekeeping (just as a computer produces "print-outs"). Some of the suggestions are terrible, some are good, a few are excellent.

Then, much in the same way that a computer processes its data, you "process" the suggestions that have been put on paper, following the special Wildcat techniques explained later in this chapter. This processing provides you with the idea or solution you are seeking.

I've used this computer analogy to demonstrate that, powerfully effective as it is, Wildcatting is simply another form of data processing. It is to your mind what a program is to a computer. In other words, it's a tried-and-tested system for accessing and manipulating data to arrive at a desired solution.

SPEEDING UP THE PROCESSING

In earlier chapters we've spoken about the subconscious, and how it processes much, if not all, of the information we may need to handle a particular problem. We've also discussed various means of accessing that information, and as you have undoubtedly noticed, the methods have been relatively slow. Effective, yes; but slow, nevertheless. Usually one must wait for the subconscious to act in its own sweet time.

Wildcatting turns the tables. It operates much closer to computer speed. During a typical Wildcat session (which, by the way, need last only ten or fifteen minutes) you'll find yourself getting ideas just as fast as you can write them down. Because many of the RAM cells feeding them to you are located in the subconscious part of your mind, in effect, Wildcatting opens up a rapid-fire connection between your subconscious and the "outside" world.

THE FIVE STEPS TO SUCCESSFUL WILDCATTING

One of the great advantages of Wildcatting is the fact that it is both easy to do and enjoyable. That's why people who have tried it apply it over and over again whenever they need innovative ideas or solutions. The procedure they follow consists of five simple steps. The names of the steps may not mean much to you at first glance, but as you continue to read, you'll quickly grasp their meanings and understand their effectiveness. Here are the five steps:

1. Mass gathering of ideas
2. Selective pruning
3. Categorizing the best ideas
4. Forming upper-level combinations
5. Checking lower-level combinations

We'll take each of these steps individually, explaining how it functions, how others have used it, and how you can put it to work in your own life.

STEP ONE: MASS GATHERING OF IDEAS

Wildcatting is a refinement of the technique developed by Alex Osborn, a New York advertising man who used to gather his employees for brainstorming sessions to get ideas for new product slogans and ad campaigns. Typically, the workers would sit around a table, hear the problem explained, and then throw out ideas willy-nilly. Out of the scores of suggestions, a few were generally found to be good.

One trouble with brainstorming was that it was not always convenient to gather a group of people, and it could be expensive in terms of time. In recent years, business and government leaders have found that one person working alone can be just as effective as a group, if he or she follows the modified system you will be shown here. As you'll see, the system also includes a special method for attracting outside ideas.

You begin the mass gathering of ideas by going to a quiet room where you won't be disturbed. At the top of a piece of paper, write a one-sentence description of the problem you want to solve or the type of idea you are seeking. This is called the Challenge, and all of the ideas you write below it will be aimed at meeting this Challenge.

Begin thinking of various possibilities that could conceivably respond to the Challenge. Forget that you know how to use judgment. As fast as the ideas come to you, write them down even if they seem farfetched. The system can only work if you are a true Wildcatter, drilling wherever your mind takes you.

Keep "drilling" until one of the following occurs:

a. You must strain for additional ideas
b. You begin to tire and your mind starts to wander
c. Twenty minutes have elapsed

Now go on to something else, perhaps your regular work. Arrange your second Wildcatting session for the next day, if you can afford to wait that long. If not, have at least three hours elapse between sessions. Begin the second session by reading over (1) the Challenge that you described at the top of the paper during the first session and (2) some of the ideas that you wrote down.

As you're reviewing the ideas, new ones will begin coming to you. (Your subconscious has been at work ever since the first session, and that's why a twenty-four hour interim period is recommended.) Repeat the procedure you followed in the first session, writing down all of the ideas, regardless of how crazy some of them might seem.

If you want still more ideas, you can get help from others. There's no need to hold a group brainstorming session. Casually mention the Challenge to one or more persons who have little or no experience or training in the particular matter. Ask for advice on the problem you are trying to solve, or for ideas of the type you are seeking.

A SPECIAL KIND OF ADVICE

The most innovative ideas often come from nonexperts in a given field. They aren't aware of rules and limitations, and thus their thinking on the matter won't be as constricted as that of the person who works with the subject every day. That's why it is important that any advice you seek comes from people who have little familiarity with the subject.

Much of the advice you get will be impractical, at least in the form it's given to you. Write it down anyway, adding it to the list of your own ideas as soon as you can. Experience has shown that six percent of not only your own ideas, but also those of others, will be practical. The freshness of the ideas obtained from nonexperts may open up promising new possibilities.

"The main obstacle to obtaining ideas from nonexperts," says product manager Tom B., "is getting rid of some of your own preconceived notions. I mean the natural inclination to pooh-pooh any idea from someone who doesn't have your own training and experience."

Tom works for an international electronics company, and his job is to develop new electronic games and toys for the firm to manufacture at its overseas plants and then import them to the United States.

"If I depended on my own expertise, or even that of the other specialists on my staff, we wouldn't have nearly as many successful products as we do," Tom explains. "We know how to design and package products, but we become so involved in it that sometimes we can lose sight of what the public really wants and will buy. So whenever I Wildcat for new product ideas I make sure I get ideas from outsiders."

Some of Tom's best ideas have come from his own children and their friends, from taxi drivers, waitresses, bartenders, and even his barber.

"When I'm Wildcatting for new product ideas, I ask them all for suggestions, and I add them to my own list. Just as often as not, the final ideas that result from the Wildcatting either originated with outsiders, or are a combintion of their thinking and my own."

Although Tom schedules formal Wildcatting sessions of fifteen or twenty minutes, during which he writes down the ideas that come to him, he also carries a small notebook with him wherever he goes.

"Some of my best ideas come not during the actual Wildcatting session," Tom explains, "but unexpectedly an hour or a day later. Having the notebook handy, I'm able to write them down before they are forgotten."

And that, of course, is another benefit provided by Wildcatting that is impossible with group brainstorming. Wildcatting allows you to benefit from your subconscious, from where some of the best ideas originate, while brainstorming is completed in one session, with no opportunity for later input.

STEP TWO: SELECTIVE PRUNING

You'll recall the advice to forget that you have judgment while you are seeking and writing down ideas. That phase of the five-step technique is purely creative, and any critical thinking can halt the flow. But once you have a good selection of ideas on paper—your own and perhaps those of others gathered over a period of at least two days—you can put your judgment back to work again. The time has come for pruning.

Read over your list of ideas, considering each one briefly. With many of them, you'll immediately see obvious faults. Write these ideas down on a fresh piece of paper and cross them off your original list. Continue this pruning procedure until you have considered every item.

PROFITING FROM "BAD" IDEAS

Why save the obviously "bad" ideas? They will continue to be useful to you when you reach one of the final steps of the Wildcatting technique. You may find then that some of them are not as bad as they seemed at first.

Judy I. chose her career by Wildcatting and, more precisely, by picking one of the items on her "reject" list.

"I had just been divorced," Judy explains, "and for someone who hasn't been employed for ten years, the job market can be a tough place. After all, what was I equipped to do except wash dishes and clean house? Well, I knew I was able to do many things, but the employers didn't."

One of the items on her "reject" list was to start her own travel agency. The idea had been rejected for many reasons, including the facts that Judy knew nothing about the travel industry and had no money to start a business.

"I had, however, always been fascinated by travel, even talking about it, and that's what prompted me to write the idea down," Judy recalls. "Of course, when it came time to prune the bad ideas from the better ones, the travel notion got scratched off the main list."

But not for long. Step Five of the Wildcatting Technique showed her how this dream might be made to come true. The result was that Judy satisfied the need for experience and start-up money by first taking a job in an existing agency. Within a year and a half, she was ready to begin her own agency in a nearby community, and it's been a successful business from the outset.

Thus at the conclusion of Step Two, you will have two lists: ideas that you believe to be worthy of further consideration, and those that seem to have little or no merit.

STEP THREE: CATEGORIZING THE BEST IDEAS

In this step, you pick the two or three best ideas on your "good" list. Just how you do this is largely a personal choice, but many people use the traditional scale-of-one-to-ten method. Simply go down the list and rate each idea on a scale of one to ten. The highest-scoring items are the ones picked for further consideration in Step Four.

"As a construction engineer, I know that rating ideas on a scale of 1 to 10 is not nearly as exact as measuring weights and distances," reports Gil M., "but the method appeals to me anyway. Just as I can rule out construction materials that are too heavy, I can rule out ideas that are too low on my scale."

Gil swears by Wildcatting, noting that he uses it almost every time a significant problem crops up on a project.

"I never cease to be amazed by the way it gives me solutions to tough problems—solutions I never would have thought of otherwise. I guess it draws out the creative instinct in me. But then the mathematical part of me gets back to work, and I rate all the ideas I've recorded, and I'm easily able to decide which of the possibilities deserve closer scrutiny."

Many people have the idea or solution they are seeking by the time they've reached this third step. Sometimes they'll have what they need by the conclusion of the first step. The full five steps are listed here for the occasions when the right ideas don't make themselves known immediately.

STEP FOUR: FORMING UPPER-LEVEL COMBINATIONS

Have you ever had what you thought was a good idea only to find, on closer examination, that there was a hitch? Practically everybody has had such experiences, and when they occur, the ideas are usually dropped. But with Wildcatting, such an idea need not and should not be dropped. You have listed so many potentially good ideas that combining two or more can open up exciting new possibilities.

In other words, if one idea has shortcomings, look for others on your list that might combine with and improve that idea. Two good ideas put together will often form a new idea that is far better than either of the originals. Consider, as an example, the pencil and the eraser. Each performs useful tasks separately, but the person who first decided to combine the two created a vastly improved product.

When you've picked an idea from your list that has major advantages and some relatively minor drawbacks, refer back to your list of other items and consider each of them one by one, but this time do it in a different light. Try to think of a way to combine the item with the idea you have already chosen. This will present new possibilities, and the odds are that you'll find a unique way to overcome whatever shortcomings might have existed.

Political consultant Sandra B. works with major candidates in many states and uses Wildcatting to deal with many of the problems she encounters. Sandra tells about how she does it:

> If, after writing down all the possibilities I can think of, one of them seems "good, but . . ." then I take that idea and write it on a separate piece of paper. Referring alternately to that piece of paper, and the paper on which the long list is written, I compare each of the items with the "good, but . . ." item, and before long, I've usually been able to create a happy marriage of ideas.
>
> My usual procedure is to write the list down at night, then sleep on it. In the morning I'm able to add several more ideas to the list, and then I start going over it. If no single idea fits the bill, I'll take the best one and begin comparing it with each of the others to find a good match. I usually can count on having a really workable solution before I go down to breakfast.
>
> My clients never cease to be amazed at my ability to take a problem they've given me late one day and present them with a great plan of action when I meet them the next morning.

STEP FIVE:
CHECKING LOWER-LEVEL COMBINATIONS

Rarely will you have completed the first four steps of the Wildcatting Technique without obtaining the idea or solution you were seeking. But on the unusual occasions when you are still without an answer, Step Five proves the value of the selective pruning you did in Step Two, when you listed the poorer ideas on a separate piece of paper.

These ideas can prove of value to you now as you check out various combinations. Take the best item on the list and, just as you did in Step Four, try combining it with one or more of the others. You may find that two relatively bad ideas can combine to form one exceptionally good one.

You'll recall that Judy I. built her career based on an idea on this "reject" list. The item she favored involved starting her own travel agency and, as you'll remember, the drawbacks were that she lacked the experience and the money to do that. Another item on the same list was the idea of taking a commissioned sales job.

"I knew that it's often easier to get a commissioned job when you have no credentials to offer an employer," Judy explains, "because you are paid in direct proportion to how well you perform. Well, when I matched this idea with the travel agency notion, they formed a tremendous combination. Why not take a commissioned job in a travel agency to get the experience I needed, see if I was cut out for that field, and build up a nest egg?"

As you know, that's what Judy did, and it led to a successful business.

HOW TO ORIGINATE DYNAMIC IDEAS
THROUGH WILDCATTING

"Is there a way to force the ideas out when they are slow in coming?"

That's a question I am often asked by people interested in Wildcatting for ideas and solutions. Sitting down with paper and pencil and writing out all the ideas that come to you is great, provided the ideas come, as they usually do. There are, however, occasions when your mind just doesn't want to co-operate, and neither your conscious nor your subconscious feeds out much information without prodding.

Prodding is precisely what you must do to speed things up. Experienced Wildcatters employ a method that is virtually guaranteed to create a full flow of ideas for their lists. They're able to churn their brains until every pertinent idea has broken loose. In other words, they don't wait for the ideas to come; they force them out.

The method they use—and it's one that should prove just as easy for you—is word association. It's almost like a game.

All you need is a book containing one or more lists of words. Many people use pocket-sized dictionaries. (The larger, shelf-sized dictionaries contain too many exotic and unfamiliar words.) Other people use Roget's Thesaurus. One person I know uses an English-French dictionary.

"I ignore the French part," he explains. "It's the Ameri-can words I'm after, and this dictionary has several thousand of the most commonly used words, and only those words."

People who are seeking ideas in a particular field or pro-fession occasionally use textbooks covering that subject. It's not the information in the textbooks they seek, but rather the selec-tion of specialized words.

THE POWER OF WORD ASSOCIATIONS

The technique is as easy as this: When you are seeking ideas and they are slow in coming, go through the list of words and associate them with the subject you are dealing with, letting each word suggest new ideas.

A powerful means of prodding your mind is to open a dictionary and see where it leads you. Here's a time-saving trick: since even a small dictionary contains thousands of words, you can often get all the associations you need by reading only the index words at the top of each page—the ones that identify the first and last words listed on that page.

For example, you might be looking for some ideas on how to raise money for an organization you belong to. Going through a dictionary, looking only at the index words printed at the top, here are some of the words you might find, along with the ideas they could give you:

Cafeteria	Dinner social
Caffeine	Coffee klatsch
Calico	Rummage sale
Carnival	
Centerboard	Sailing regatta
Clean	Car wash
Contest	Game social or raffle
Correspondence	Fund appeal by mail
Cowboy	Rodeo

If you can get all these ideas just by going through the "C" section of the dictionary, imagine all the ideas you'd have by thumbing through the entire book!

Obviously, not every word is going to have a usable association. Give every word a chance, though. Spend ten or fifteen seconds with each word you encounter, thinking of possible relationships between it and your main subject. Sometimes words that would seem to have no immediate connection can lead to a valuable idea. That's because the mind relates one thought to another in an unpredictable way.

ONE WORD LEADS TO SEVERAL IDEAS

The word "name" led the operator of a struggling mail-order business to expand it into a hugely profitable enterprise. Dennis T. had been selling novelties through magazine ads and small catalogs.

"The income barely matched the outgo," Dennis says, "and I was getting very little, if anything, for all the effort I was devoting to it. There was no trouble increasing sales volume, but the increased income always seemed to be matched by higher costs. Then I read an article on Wildcatting and became fascinated with the possibilities of word associations. I opened a small dictionary to the 'N' section and began associating."

One of the words he encountered was "name," and this caused him to think of the name of his business and to speculate that a more dramatic name might help. He wrote that idea down. Then, as he continued to think about the word "name," the thought associations led in a new direction. What about the names on his customer list? As in any mail-order business, they were his most valuable asset because whenever a catalog is sent out, people who have bought before are more likely to buy again.

"And if names are valuable to me, aren't they valuable to every mail-order company?" That's a question Dennis asked himself as he wrote down this idea: sell or rent names.

Later, as he went over the dozens of ideas on his list, Dennis realized that selling or renting names had the biggest potential. There are thousands of direct-mail operations in the United States that will pay top dollar for the rental of good mailing lists. They need the names of proven mail-order buyers. (Names taken from such things as a telephone book are next to useless because, in order for an advertising campaign to be successful, the ads must be sent to people who are known to have purchased similar products through the mail.)

"Here was a way that expanding my own novelty sales business could pay off," Dennis explains. "Even though my direct profits failed to increase when I increased sales, the number of names on my customer list did grow. It stood to reason that, the more names of proven novelty buyers I could add to my list, the more names I could rent to other mail-order companies. So I went ahead and expanded my sales business, even though I knew it would be on a break-even basis."

Break-even, that is, until he had gathered enough names to begin renting them on a large scale. At $60 per thousand names, large checks from other companies began rolling in. The last time I spoke with Dennis, he had 350,000 names on his list. Thus every time he rents the entire list, he receives $21,000 minus the ten percent commission he pays to the list broker who finds rental customers for him.

Since the list is rented at least three times per month, his net profit from name rentals is $50,000 to $60,000 per month.

"If I hadn't used word association, I'd probably still be struggling along with little or no profit at all," Dennis comments.

GIVE YOURSELF A LOT TO CHOOSE FROM

When you see a particularly beautiful photograph on a calendar, or a powerful news photo on the front page of your newspaper, do you think it was outstanding skill that enabled the photographer to capture that shot? Perhaps. But bear in mind that he, too, was Wildcatting. You can be sure he took dozens (perhaps even hundreds) of shots just to get the one that is so impressive. What works for the photographer with pictures will also work for you with ideas. Give yourself a big selection to choose from, and you'll wind up with a much better final choice.

HOW TO DISCOVER POWERFUL SOLUTIONS THROUGH WILDCATTING

Word association is most effective when you need to think up new ideas. But when it comes to solving specific problems, there is another Wildcatting method that many people find more effective.

Like word association, this method involves a special kind of mind-prodding. Instead of looking at lists of words to prod your thinking, however, the idea is to use the problem itself to do the prodding.

When you have been able to think of only a few options for dealing with a problem (and the success of Wildcatting depends on a wide variety to choose from) here's how to think of many more: alter the problem. Write down a way of solving the initial problem by creating a new one. The fact is, you'll be able to write down many ways.

"Whoa, hold on there, halt!" I can hear you protesting. You complain that there is no advantage in solving a problem by creating a new one. Ah, but there is. One of the new problems you create may be much easier to solve than the problem you began with.

Let's see how this method works. We'll imagine that you have stopped at one side of a footbridge that has washed out, and you need to get to the other side of the stream that the bridge formerly crossed. The problem, obviously, is the washed-out bridge. Just as obvious is the fact that it's impossible to solve the problem; you are not able to repair the bridge by yourself within a reasonable time.

So, using the Alternative Problem Method, you think of other ways of getting across the stream, and you write all of them down—even if they pose new problems. Here are some of the alternatives you might put on your list:

ALTERNATIVE	NEW PROBLEM IT WOULD CREATE
Swim across the stream	You would get your clothes wet
Build a small raft	This would take a lot of time
Find a shallow area and wade across	It might be hard to find
Go to another bridge downstream	It is ten miles away
Tie a rope to a branch, swing across	You don't have a rope

Obviously, some of the problems posed by these alternatives are just as difficult to deal with as the original. But one or two have some possibilities. Taking off your shoes and wading across is one; tying a rope to a branch and swinging across is another (if you're young and agile). True, the first option would require finding a shallow area and the second would require you to locate a rope, but these problems are easier to deal with than the original one.

I'm sure you get the point. It's a lot easier to think of imperfect problem-solving options than it is to think of perfect ones. In the course of a twenty-minute Wildcatting session, you should be able to put dozens on your list. Each of these will pose its own new problem, but when you review the list, you're likely to find some of the alternatives much easier to handle.

Too many people are poor problem-solvers because they demand perfect solutions, which are few and far between. By substituting an easy-to-solve problem for a more difficult one, you can deal with almost any situation.

TOUGH SITUATIONS MADE EASIER

Andy K. is the business manager of a traveling theatrical company that performs at civic centers, college field houses, and auditoriums across the country.

"You can imagine the problems I have to face," Andy says. "If one of the key performers becomes ill, or we get delayed by weather, or some of our equipment fails to arrive, we're in a lot of trouble."

But not nearly as much trouble as they would be in if Andy didn't use Wildcatting and, more specifically, the Alternative Problem Method.

"I sit down with paper and pencil and can usually list fifteen or twenty alternatives in as many minutes," Andy explains. "Out of this many, one or two are bound to be workable, and I've found a viable way to carry on with our schedule."

In explaining his use of Wildcatting, Andy is emphatic about one thing.

"When I start thinking of alternatives to put on paper, I don't concern myself with the new problems they might present. I write them down as soon as they occur to me, without allowing any criticism of the ideas to enter my mind. As soon as one alternative is written down, I move on to the next. My goal is to get as many on paper as I possibly can, within a reasonable period of time."

Like thousands of other Wildcatters, Andy has learned that one of the key rules is to forbid criticism during the list-making process. They know that criticism inhibits the flow of ideas and solutions.

Now that you, too, know the rules of successful Wildcatting, you have added a powerful new tool to your arsenal of Mental Leverage weapons.

—9—

How to Fine-Tune
Your Listening Powers

A colleague and I both covered a press conference called by a household products firm to unveil a new product. As we left the meeting room together, my colleague commented, "It looks like this company has a hot product there. I'd say its financial future is assured."

"To the contrary," I said, "I believe that company is in trouble. I wouldn't be surprised if it shuts down this factory within the year."

When my colleague asked what caused me to believe that, I explained: "From what you and I both heard at the press conference today."

He was flabbergasted. Three or four months later, when the plant was indeed shut down, he recalled our conversation.

"How did you know?" he asked. "What did you hear that I didn't hear?"

By the time you're finished reading this chapter, you'll have a good idea of what I heard and, more important, you'll know how I listened to it.

Most adults use only a small part of their listening ability. Their hearing may be perfectly normal, enabling them to detect all kinds of sounds, but they miss much of the significance of what they hear.

That's why two people who attend the same meeting may come away with far different impressions, depending on how well-tuned their listening powers are. One of them will hear only what was said and take it literally. The other is able to glean much more.

The difference between hearing and listening is like the difference between looking at a text in which many of the sentences are printed in an unfamiliar language and reading one printed in your native tongue. You see the ink marks on the paper, but it takes training to understand what all of them mean.

When you expand your own ability to listen, you'll begin to reap many benefits. You will:

* Obtain valuable information that other people miss
* Understand the hidden meanings behind what people say
* Recognize the signals people unwittingly give
* Get more from people than they want to reveal

Nations spend billions of dollars on what is termed intelligence—learning what other countries are up to. Corporations spend millions on research, learning what their customers (and potential customers) want and will pay for. Just as nations benefit from intelligence and corporations benefit from research, individuals can benefit from learning more about (and from) their fellow human beings, and it doesn't cost a penny.

Wouldn't you, for example, like to know:

* Whether your boss believes you deserve a raise?
* What someone of the opposite sex thinks of you?
* About big opportunities that are known to only a few?
* How much a customer is willing to pay for your product?
* Which people really do like you?
* Why you didn't get that promotion you were hoping for?
* What people who make vague statements really mean?
* What most impresses (or turns off) someone important to you?

These are just some of the benefits to be gained from fine-tuning your listening powers—a Mental Leverage skill that will give you new insights and a lot of profitable knowledge.

HEAR ALL THAT YOU CHOOSE TO HEAR

The phrase "in one ear and out the other" is an apt one in describing what happens to most of the sounds that surround us. We have trained ourselves to ignore sounds that are not important. Although we hear the sounds, we pay them no heed.

On the other hand, if a particular type of sound is of special interest, we develop the ability to hear it more acutely than other people can. An orchestra conductor, for example, can often single out the musician who played a bad note. There may have been many other musical sounds in the room that he heard simultaneously, but he's able to pinpoint precisely where the bad sound came from.

A college psychology class conducted a sidewalk experiment in which students would drop coins on the pavement to determine the reaction of passersby. When the dropped coin was a penny or a dime, most people kept on walking. When it was a fifty-cent piece, the majority turned and looked. They obviously knew the difference in the sound. But what particularly interested the class was an unplanned result of the experiment.

One of the students mistakenly dropped several coins. A man who happened to be walking by helped her retrieve them. When the student thought that all had been collected, the man suggested they keep looking.

"You dropped two quarters, a dime, and three pennies," he said, "and we haven't located one of the quarters yet."

"How do you know what I dropped?" she asked.

"I heard them hit the pavement. I know the sounds of different coins. Try it yourself sometime. They're not hard to learn."

The orchestra conductor and the pedestrian had trained themselves to interpret sounds that most people miss. The same can be done with the meaning behind what people say. You can train yourself to interpret words and statements so that

you obtain highly useful information that escapes nearly everyone else.

HOW TO GAIN VALUABLE INFORMATION THAT OTHERS MISS

We're going to be dealing with methods of interpreting
hidden meanings, interpersonal signals, and information that
others don't want to reveal, but first there are some basics to
consider. These are the basics of gaining a better understanding
of what is said to you. Simple as the methods are, many people
fail to use them much of the time. As a result, most people only
retain about one-fourth of what they hear. A good deal of
valuable information is lost that way.

*The First Basic: Concentrate on content rather than
delivery.* Annoying mannerisms, faulty English, or self-puffery;
any of these can turn us off from a speaker. We are bothered so
much by *how* something is said that the message bypasses us
entirely. Political leaders know this, and that's why they try to
pick candidates with "charisma," or high personal appeal. By
paying more attention to charm than to what they stand for, we
are often disappointed with how candidates perform after they
take office.

Paying more atention to style than to content can lead us
down either of two wrong streets. The first one steers us away
from valuable information that could help us. The second
causes us to take people at face value, accepting what they say
without question. This can be expensive.

While Ben D. was waiting for sales help in an appliance
store, he listened as the salesman touted a certain video cassette recorder to a young couple. It was a higher-priced model,
and the salesman, a fatherly type, assured the couple that, with
all its fancy features, it was the best buy. They plunked down a
charge card and bought it with hardly a question asked.

When it was his turn, Ben said that he, too, was looking
for a VCR. The salesman repeated his statement about the expensive model's attractive features, and his demeanor seemed
to say, "Now would I, a man much like your own father, steer
you wrong?"

Ben found himself about to do what the couple had done: go for broke and buy the fully loaded model. But then, remembering the first basic of effective listening, he began thinking about what the salesman had actually said. Surprise! Ben could easily do without the options the man was trying to peddle. In fact, they had no appeal at all to him, since Ben is not interested in watching the nightly news in slow motion, fast motion, or stop motion. Ben doesn't even want to skip over the commercials, because they provide excellent opportunities to take a break.

"Big Daddy" had almost cost Ben $375 more than he needed to pay. As soon as Ben realized that he was putting too much blind trust in the salesman's paternal advice, he began paying more attention to content rather than style, and realized that he was being offered stuff he didn't want.

The Second Basic: Keep an open mind. If you argue with what is being said (even if the arguments are mental and kept to yourself) you'll be blocking out a good deal of information, some of which could be valuable. Too often we're tempted to think, "That's all foolishness," and then we turn off the speaker and start daydreaming. Or, we disagree vocally with the speaker, stopping him in his tracks.

A real estate broker tells of the time he ran into an old acquaintance on the street and, after exchanging information on how each other's children were doing, the friend told the broker that he had taken up a new religion.

"It sounded like one of those weird cults to me," the broker recalls, "and the more he said about it, the more I tuned him out. A few weeks later, I read in the newspaper that his group had just bought an old church. That church had been under Multiple Listing. I could have sold it to them just as easily as the broker who actually made the sale. Had I paid more attention to my friend, I might have learned they were in the market for a building, and the sale would have been mine."

It's wise to remember that even when you disagree with what somebody is telling you, there may be chunks of helpful information in what the other person says.

The Third Basic: Interrupt the smart way. You've been brought up to believe that it's rude to interrupt. One type of interruption, however, is not only acceptable, it's welcomed by the speaker as a sign of your interest in what he's saying. When you ask questions, the speaker knows you're paying attention and he is also given a feeling of importance. Your asking questions implies he knows something that you don't, and this makes him an authority, even if the topic is a minor one. As a result, he speaks to you with more interest and enthusiasm.

Felix P. attended a seminar on the development of listening skills, and he began utilizing this Third Basic almost immediately. He credits it with locking in a new career for him. Felix was sixty at the time he attended the seminar. A month later, due to circumstances beyond his control, he was dismissed by the company for which he had worked twenty-two years.

A sixty-year-old jobless man has a tough time finding work, especially if he's been in the $50,000-a-year bracket and he wants to stay there. Despite laws against age discrimination, employers can find all kinds of excuses for not hiring someone.

"After being turned down for a dozen jobs in my own field, I decided to try for work in a slightly different field, but which still required the skills and contacts I had developed over the years," Felix explains. "I arranged interviews with several firms in this new field, and at each interview I was candid about my lack of direct experience.

"In one of the sessions, the interviewer began telling me how different the job requirements were from anything I'd done before. I asked many questions pertaining to what she was saying, and, frankly, I learned a lot. If nothing else, I realized that the knowledge I gained from her answers would help me in future interviews."

But future interviews were not needed. Felix's asking questions so impressed the interviewer that he got the job.

She told him, "You're the first applicant to express a lot of interest in the work itself; most people inquire mainly about the pay and benefits. It would be a shame if we missed someone as vitally interested as you."

So it can be smart to interrupt by asking pertinent questions. Not only will you obtain more helpful and interesting information, you may also score valuable points with the other person.

The Fourth Basic: Learn to ignore distractions. If you want to gain valuable information that other people miss, then learn to do what most of them haven't learned to do: ignore physical distractions. There are proven techniques to help you do this, and applying these techniques will give you an advantage over other listeners.

First, you can take notes—whether you need them or not. Nothing is more effective in keeping your attention aimed at the subject and away from outside stimuli then having to write down all the key points. It's the technique to use when you're one of a group listening to a speaker.

Second, you can play games—really. When you want to be sure your mind is pinned to what the speaker is saying, set up mental challenges for yourself. For example: pick the longest word in each sentence the speaker says. Or another example, since you can think three or four times as fast as the other person can talk, use the extra time to mentally reword some of his sentences. See if you can summarize the same thoughts in fewer words.

And third, you can use the memory techniques given in Chapter 2 to file away the key points made by the speaker. This will have the dual benefit of keeping you so busy that it locks out distractions, while it also ensures that the new information stays with you.

Twelve workers in a regional office of a federal agency were sent to Washington to attend a seminar on upgrading their skills. Unfortunately, renovations were being made to the building where the seminar was being given and it was easy for the people attending to be distracted. Because of the noise and confusion, it would be safe to say that most of them did not get all they could have from the seminar.

At least one of them, however, was familiar with the techniques of ignoring distractions that you've just seen. As Warren T. explains it, "I took notes, played games, and used a variety of memory techniques to make sure I heard and retained the material being taught us. As a result, when the twelve of us took a Civil Service exam a few months later, I scored the highest."

You've now seen the four Basics of gaining valuable information that others miss. Practice them daily. They'll bring a dramatic improvement to your listening effectiveness. They also pave the way for the unusual techniques you are about to learn.

DECODING HIDDEN MEANINGS BEHIND WHAT PEOPLE SAY

Most of us were brought up to think one thing and say another. It's called being "civilized" or "grown up."

Young children almost always say precisely what they mean, but as they add a few years they learn that there are "nicer" ways of saying certain things, and that other things are best left unsaid. A child of five will announce loudly, for all to hear, that he has to go to the bathroom, while one a few years older has learned to be more discreet about it. There can also be an awkward period when a youngster hasn't yet learned that some thoughts, even when couched in nice terms, should not be expressed, such as the time my six-year-old niece announced to a gathering of adult relatives: "I itch in the pubic area."

By the time children reach their teens, they are very conscious of what other people think of them, and they begin to be especially careful about what they say and how they say it. It's a habit they carry throughout their lives. To avoid making a poor impression or offending someone, they rarely say precisely what they think. That's why it can be dangerous to take even the most honorable person at his word. We human beings are too civilized to be totally honest.

Even when we act in a supposedly uncivilized manner, such as speaking in anger, we're not as blunt as we might appear. Our real motives are often left unsaid, and the cause of our anger may not be what it appears to be.

Thus, almost every statement we make has at least two meanings: the obvious meaning and one or more hidden meanings. I call them the overt meaning and the covert meaning. Two dictionary definitions might be helpful:

OVERT: Open and easily observable.

COVERT: Not open or easily observable.

For example, a person may say: "I don't enjoy going to parties where most of the people are strangers to me." That's an overt statement. It's easily understandable and to the point. But, it also has a covert meaning. Without saying it, the person has indicated that he or she does not find it easy or pleasant to strike up conversations with strangers. The person has said, covertly, "I am shy."

Your boss may say: "You work so hard, it doesn't really bother me that you were thirty-five minutes late today." That's the overt statement, but covertly the boss has told you something else. He noticed that you were thirty-five minutes late. If it didn't really matter, he would not have noticed it or commented on it, and certainly he would not have been so precise about the time.

There are two important advantages you can gain if you learn how to decode the hidden meanings behind what people say.

HOW HIDDEN MEANINGS CAN HELP YOU

"All that stuff about overt and covert meanings is interesting," people are apt to say to me, "but of what use is it? Why try to decode the hidden meaning behind what someone else says?"

The answer is that your future depends on it. The added knowledge you obtain can boost your career, enhance your business success, and help you achieve any other goals you have. Imagine what it can do for you in just these two areas:

* NEGOTIATING. If you stop to think about it, you'll realize that your day is full of negotiations. They cover everything from trivial matters (such as getting your young child to eat his spinach) to important affairs (such as convincing a prospective employer you're the person for an important job). The covert meanings behind what the other person says to you provide important clues as to how you can win the negotiation.

* INSIDE INFORMATION. The average person never hears about the best jobs, business and investment opportunities, bargain offerings, and many other desirable things.

Although people who know about outstanding opportunities rarely talk about them openly, they often unwittingly tip their hands to those who understand the covert meanings of what they say.

While the purpose of this book is not to teach you how to win negotiations or land a job, it brings those goals much closer to achievement by showing how to leverage your mental powers so that you perform much better than your competitors. Decoding hidden meanings is one of the important skills in the Mental Leverage inventory. Let's see how this skill is applied, first in negotiations and then in uncovering inside information.

HOW TO GAIN IMPORTANT NEGOTIATING CLUES

If there's ever a time when people don't say what they mean, it's during negotiations. A good negotiator (whether he's a used car salesman, a labor contract bargainer, or a child seeking permission to stay up late) often covers up what he's really thinking. The negotiator wants to get the biggest possible concession from you by granting the fewest possible concessions himself, and the more information he reveals, the weaker his position becomes.

On the other hand, he must appear to be open and friendly so that he can win your trust. Thus he develops the knack of seeming to speak candidly, without actually revealing any information that will help you. Fortunately for you, the more he talks the more he unwittingly reveals.

People who practice Mental Leverage know there are certain "flag words" to listen for in any type of negotiations. The flag words fit into three different categories, and whenever you hear them during negotiations, you have a good indication that the speaker is not speaking the truth, the whole truth, and nothing but the truth. Here are the flag words to look for:

* OF COURSE, NATURALLY, NO DOUBT: When a negotiator precedes a statement with any of these phrases, the degree of certainty is far lower than he would like you to believe. If, for example, a car salesman says, "Of course, that's the lowest price I can offer the car for," he's really willing to bargain some more. If a prospective

employer says, "No doubt we can give you a raise after six months," he really means there is significant doubt.

* BY THE WAY, INCIDENTALLY: The objective is to make a statement seem like a minor point, but the opposite is usually the case. "By the way, this job involves some night work," is tossed in as a trivial matter, but it's actually important. Another example: "Incidentally, this mother-daughter house is in a one-family residential zone, but the zoning board has overlooked it so far." That's not incidental at all.

* I CAN'T BECAUSE . . . : Whenever a negotiator takes great pains to tell you why he can't give you a certain concession, you can be sure it's a concession he *can* give. He's merely trying to dissuade you from seeking it. "I can't lower the price because my boss would kill me" means "Sure, if you bargain hard enough, I'll come down some more." Also, "I can't pay you any more because it would throw our budget out of whack" means "Sure, I could pay you more, but you're going to have to show me why I should." Rule of thumb: The more the negotiator tries to explain, the less sincere he is about what he "can't" do.

While there are no specific flag words that let you know precisely when a negotiator has reached his limit and will offer no further concessions, there is an important clue to watch for, and that is a sudden change in attitude. When a negotiator does any of the following, it is probably a signal that he's at the end of his rope:

* Drops the first name basis and becomes more formal in addressing you ("Mr. Johnson" instead of "Joe")
* Becomes abrupt in his attitude
* Looks at his watch repeatedly
* Appears to lose interest in the conversation
* Allows his mind to wander
* Stops trying to sell you his side of the issue

As long as the negotiator appears to be vitally interested in working out a deal, you can be sure there's room for more give and take. When signals such as those listed above start to appear, you know that you've won as much as you're apt to.

HOW TO DECODE INSIDE INFORMATION

The method used to decode hidden or covert meanings is known as Content Analysis. Governments apply it to determine what each other's communiqués really mean; businesses use it to decipher consumer attitudes and discover what competitors are planning; and experts in Mental Leverage use it in their daily dealings with other people. Although we'll be referring mostly to verbal communications such as conversations and speeches, it can also be used to unravel the covert meanings of written communications and documents.

Content Analysis reveals hidden meanings by looking at the frequency and use of certain words and expressions. When a person uses a particular word or expression frequently, that's a clear indicator of what's on his mind.

I'll bet that without realizing it, you've applied Content Analysis many times. For example, when someone begins to speak often about another person, you have a good idea that a deep interest in that other person is developing. Your teen-aged son may date several girls, but if he refers to one more than the others, you can count on her being his heartthrob. When you call a busy plumber or electrician and he indicates "maybe" he can come tomorrow "if" he's "able" to finish another job on time, you have a fairly good indication from all those qualifying words that you won't be seeing him for several days at the least.

At the press conference mentioned at the beginning of this chapter, it was Content Analysis that enabled me to predict correctly that the company was in trouble. As I recall, here are some of the statements I heard:

* ★ "This product will restore our leadership in the field."
* ★ "With the success of this product, we can once again be a leading employer and taxpayer in this community."
* ★ "We'll be able to return our labor force to full strength."
* ★ "We're fully anticipating a turnaround situation."

* "This product will fit in nicely, replacing other products that are being discontinued from our line."
* "With the economy expected to improve, we think the demand for this type of product will be restored to its former levels."

Any of the above statements made alone would not be much of a signal. But when all six are uttered at the same press conference, a big red flag is being waved. In six different ways, we were told that the company was down on its luck but it hoped things would soon pick up. Perhaps you detected the flag-waving words:

"will restore our leadership"

"we can once again"

"we'll be able to return"

"a turnaround situation"

"products that are being discontinued"

"will be restored"

What you see above is the same message expressed in six different ways. The company has hit bad times, but it hopes a new product will reverse the tide. At the news conference, these statements were not expressed one right after another. They were spread out over a period of about an hour, and that's why reporters unfamiliar with Content Analysis did not become aware of the company's problems. So much was said bearing no hint of those problems that the significance of these six statements escaped most people.

Mental Leverage had taught me, however, about Content Analysis. I knew that inside information is often unwittingly revealed by people who make similar statements over and over again. That's precisely what happened here, enabling me to detect the "trouble" theme that the other reporters missed.

THE KEY TO SUCCESS IN CONTENT ANALYSIS

Content Analysis enables you to pick up unexpected "signals" from what people say. You gain information the other person did not intend to reveal because you know how to detect repeated themes in the conversation or speech.

But you don't have to wait for unexpected signals. The key to outstanding success in Content Analysis is knowing in advance what you are listening for.

I can hear you protesting. "Wait a minute," you say. "How can I know what I'm listening for when I have no idea what the inside information is?"

The answer is that if you are prepared by knowing the general type of information that would be helpful to you—not necessarily the specifics—you'll find it much easier to pick up any signals inadvertently dropped by the speaker.

When I covered that press conference, for example, I was looking for an unusual angle. The purpose of the conference was to announce a new product, but since everyone else would be reporting that, I wanted something different. Realizing that the company was an important employer and taxpayer in the community, I decided to listen for information about the company itself, rather than being interested just in its new product. That's how I picked up the repeated signals about the firm's difficulties.

CAREER-BUILDING WITH CONTENT ANALYSIS

A friend of mine is highly ambitious. She works in a major metropolitan bank and, as she says, "I didn't want to wait until almost retirement age to begin making good money." Maria has been helped in her career by many of the skills spelled out in Mental Leverage. She credits one of them, Content Analysis, with making her a vice-president.

"It was at a staff meeting," she recalls. "I entered the meeting with the goal of picking up any information that might lead to new opportunities for me within the bank. During the conference, one of the senior vice-presidents was asked about a particular problem, and he replied that we should not be concerned about it, because provisions were being made to handle it in a new way.

"This naturally caused my ears to perk up. What new way? Well, a few minutes later, this same executive referred to some office space that was being set aside for a new project.

And, just before closing the meeting, he suggested that if we had any friends at other banks we should have them get in touch with our personnel department because there might soon be some administrative openings.

"One plus one plus one equals three, and in this case, three meant that a new division was being opened at our bank. To me, and probably to me alone, that was obvious from what the senior vice-president had said. He had told us that new work functions were being created, office space was being set aside for a new project, and new hiring would be done. Do you know what I did? I put in for an immediate transfer to the staff of that senior vice-president. I wanted to be in on the ground floor of the new project, realizing that whatever it was, it would offer unusual opportunities for growth and advancement."

Grow and advance Maria did. The department involved overseas operations, an exciting new field for her. Shortly after her transfer she was named a supervisor, and a year after that she was appointed a vice-president.

"I was the only one attending that staff conference who acted on the statements dropped offhandedly by the senior vice-president," Maria says. "And I was also the only one of that group to be promoted so rapidly. I thank Content Analysis for that."

BUILD POPULARITY AND PRESTIGE BY HEEDING INTERPERSONAL SIGNALS

Most of our discussion in this chapter so far has dealt with improving listening skills for the sake of gaining additional information. There's another benefit that many people overlook. Being a skilled listener helps build your own popularity and prestige.

One of the easiest ways to win other people's friendship and admiration is to listen carefully to what they say. It's human nature—people love to be listened to. They want the person they're speaking with to hear everything they are saying and understand their point of view. Good listeners are worth their weight in gold, because the effort put forth will be returned many times over.

For example, did you know that when you listen well, the other person rewards you by paying closer attention to what you say? A proven method of making another person more receptive to your ideas is to begin by hearing him out.

That's how a good friend of mine, Helen O., got a free trip to Europe for her daughter, Amy. A civic organization was sending a group of twenty youngsters on a two-week exchange visit. The children going on the trip were chosen by school administrators. Amy was not on the original list.

"When I asked the principal why," Helen says, "he explained that although Amy was the type of child they would like to have included on the trip, there were far more applicants than available slots. When I asked if she could be placed on the standby list, he agreed, but pointed out that a number of other children were already on standby.

"Then I remembered what I had learned about the benefits of being a good listener. The principal seemed overwhelmed with the work of preparing for the overseas trip, and I made a remark about the pressure he obviously was feeling. As he related all of the tasks he was facing in connection with this project in addition to his regular work, I gave him my complete attention and interest.

"It was obvious that he appreciated being able to let off steam, especially with such a good listener. Then, after about fifteen minutes, he paused and said, 'Tell me why this trip is so important to Amy.'

"I've never seen it fail! When you want to get a point across to somebody, the best way to break the ice is to listen first to what he has to say. When he's through, he'll either turn the conversation your way or be receptive when you do so.

"I explained that Amy's grandparents had come from the country to be visited in Europe, and that I'd like her to know more about her heritage. The principal made no promises, but several days later, when one of the children had to cancel out of the trip because of illness in the family, Amy was picked as the replacement."

As Helen proved, skilled listening does more than make you better informed. It's a powerful tool in winning your way with others.

HOW TO GET INFORMATION FROM THOSE WHO DON'T WANT TO GIVE IT TO YOU

You can listen forever, but it will do little good if there's nothing to listen to. That's why I include, as one of the skills of good listening, the knack of getting other people to talk about things they'd rather not discuss. Information you gain this way can make a tremendous difference in your life and career.

There are proven ways to elicit important information from people who don't want to give it to you. Of course, I'm talking about completely honorable methods. We'll leave eavesdropping and torture to the spies. The proven methods I refer to let people willingly and, yes, enthusiastically, tell you what you want to know.

There's nothing secret about these methods. They're used every day by skilled investigators, news reporters, personnel directors, and people in other fields whose job it is to elicit needed information. What techniques professionals use in their work, you can use to obtain information that will help you advance in your career. You don't have to be an investigator to benefit from getting early word on job openings, business opportunities, and investment windfalls.

What does a trained investigator, news reporter, lawyer, or job interviewer do when the person being interviewed fails to volunteer the needed information? A two-step process is followed:

1. The professional switches to a topic the other person is willing to discuss, getting him in a talkative, enthusiastic mood.
2. While the other person is still talkative and enthusiastic, the professional steers the topic toward the "fringes" of what he really wants to discuss.

Almost invariably, the other person begins to volunteer more and more information about the "forbidden" topic, and before long, you've obtained all that you want to know. By getting the person to discuss a subject he's enthusiastic about, you've disarmed him. Then, by steering the topic gently in the direction of what you wish to know, the steamroller effect that you've established keeps him talking.

I have a letter from a man whose salary was tripled within a year because he used this technique. Ted C. had read an article I wrote on this aspect of Mental Leverage, and he decided to apply it at the next opportunity, which came very soon. Here's how Ted relates what happened:

> The company where I work is small and tightly knit, loaded with people who have a lot more seniority than I. There aren't many opportunities for advancement for the simple reason that in most departments there are many people already on the waiting list. Usually, in such circumstances, the best way to advance is to switch to another company. But, because of family obligations, I'm tied down to the community where I live, and there are no other similar firms nearby.

> I decided that, in a company where so many people were ahead of me on the seniority list, the only way to advance was to jump ahead of them in terms of skills the company needed. So I went to the top man and asked him what I could do to make myself more valuable to the company. He wasn't very helpful, telling me just to keep on doing the good work I was doing. Obviously, he wasn't as ambitious for me as I was.

> Then I remembered the technique of getting information from those who don't want to give it. I got the boss talking about his own job and all the responsibilities that went with it. People are eager to talk about how important and hard-working they are, and he was no exception. Gently, I steered the topic to the problems he faced. I asked what the most irksome problems were, and he identified them.

> By the time I left his office, I knew what my career-advancement steps should be. The boss had volunteered that one of his biggest problems was finding qualified people to help supervise the night shift. Mind you, when I asked him outright what I could do to advance myself, he had been noncommittal. He just couldn't picture me in any job other than what I was doing. But, a few moments later, thanks to my prodding, he was telling me where he badly needed qualified people.

A day or two later, I went to the personnel department and offered to switch to the night shift, if a supervisory job were open. Of course a supervisory job was
open, and of course I got it. There was an immediate advancement in pay, and because few people were ahead of
me on the waiting list, there were frequent advancements
in rank. I am now the overall night supervisor, earning
three times what I made that day when I got the boss to
spill the beans.

It's only human nature that most other people don't have
the same concern for your future as you have, and thus, when
you seek information that could help you, they often are not as
cooperative as you'd like them to be. Ted found this out when
he spoke with the company bigwig.

The next time—and every time—you encounter someone
who declines to offer the helpful information you seek, apply
the technique you've learned here. When a person won't talk
about what interests you, get him talking and enthusiastic
about what interests him. Then, gently steer the conversation
toward what you really want to know. You'll have started a
steamroller that will keep on rolling until you've obtained all
the information you need.

—10—

Use Mental Leverage to Control Other People

The early chapters of this book revealed that one of the most powerful ways to outperform other people is to use a greater proportion of your brainpower than they are using of theirs. This chapter shows how the same principle that allows you to outsmart other people also gives you the power to control your actions.

You're going to learn how Mental Leverage will give you the upper hand over others and:

* Get them to do almost anything for you
* Resolve disagreements in your favor
* Make your own viewpoints stand out
* Make a great impression on people who can help you

"I found, a long time ago, that you don't actually have to be smarter than other people in order to get them to act and think the way you want them to," says self-made millionaire Ken C. "Heck, I never did well in school, and from my IQ test results, my teachers never saw much potential for me. It wasn't until after I left school and learned some of the techniques now known as Mental Leverage that success began rolling my way."

Ken, who owns a chain of restaurants, is the first to admit that his ability in handling other people is no greater than anyone else's.

"It's just that I've learned how to make better use of it than most other people have," Ken explains.

Leveraging his ability to control the thinking and actions of others enabled Ken to build his restaurant empire. By making better use of the ability all of us have to influence people, Ken was able to:

* Persuade a bank to give him one hundred percent financing for his first restaurant
* Convince a city agency to change the zoning of the restaurant site
* Steal the top chef from the city's largest hotel
* Attract crowds of patrons to the new establishment
* Quickly gain a great reputation
* Build on his first success to establish a chain of steak houses

You have the same potential to influence others that Ken has. This chapter shows how you can develop it to the fullest, so that you, too, can win the confidence and support of other people in achieving your highest goals.

THE SECRET BEHIND TRUE POWER

Power is a trade-off. You get other people to do what you want by giving them something that they want. Mental Leverage proves that what you give can be very, very small in comparison to what you get in return.

The first thing you must realize is that no one does anything he doesn't want to do. An employee, even one who hates his job, would rather go to work and earn a salary than stay home and be broke. A mugging victim wants to turn over his money because that's better than being hurt or even killed. A person who donates to charity does so for a reward: the good feeling it gives him.

There you have a hint of how Mental Leverage enables you to wield true power over other people. You have, in fact, learned the first rule for gaining instant mastery over others:

The quickest way to motivate people is to understand that everything they do is really aimed at pleasing themselves.

Every action made by each of us is performed to fill a

physical or emotional need. We work at our jobs in order to pay for food and shelter; we go to church to improve our spiritual well-being; we do volunteer work at the local hospital because it gives us a feeling of warmth when we help others; we run for office in a civic organization because it gives us a feeling of importance.

One of the foremost emotional needs is the final one mentioned in the paragraph above—a feeling of importance. There is not a human being anywhere who does not crave importance of one type or other. It can, in fact, be said that virtually everything we do is done to make ourselves feel more important. Even the person who, "out of the goodness of his heart," donates time or money to charity is really doing it because being able to help others adds to his feeling of importance.

This leads us to the second rule for gaining instant mastery over others:

> You can get anyone to do almost anything if it makes him feel important.

That's the trade-off I've been talking about. You don't have to pay cash, you don't have to threaten a person with bodily harm, and you certainly don't have to beg him to do your bidding. All you need do is arrange it so that he gains a feeling of importance by doing what you want him to do.

What does it require on your part? Just a sentence or two.

VERBAL TECHNIQUES THAT GIVE YOU INSTANT MASTERY OVER OTHERS

People who are new to the personal power techniques of Mental Leverage are almost always amazed at the difference a few words can make. It's the difference between merely asking someone to do something for you and wording your request in such a way that he is compelled to do it because it makes him feel more important.

People will go to great lengths to:

* Gain a bit of self esteem
* Live up to a good reputation
* Demonstrate that they are needed

* Meet a challenge
* Prove their superiority

In each of these cases, and in many others I could name, what the person is really seeking is a feeling of importance. When you can supply that for him, you become his master. You get a lot of what you want by giving him a little of what he wants.

In my book, *Control Dynamics for Mastery Over People*, I point out that giving the other person a feeling of importance (FOI) can work wonders in just about any situation, even in getting a policeman to tear up a traffic ticket. The book relates the experience of a business client of mine—a man to whom I had explained the power of FOI.

An hour or two after I had told Frank about FOI, he called me on the phone and spoke in a voice that betrayed his excitement.

"It really works!" Frank said. "Remember how I cut short our meeting to make a bank deposit? Well, my haste got me a speeding ticket. I was stopped for going forty-five in a thirty-mile-an-hour zone."

Frank had been stopped for speeding before, but he had never been able to talk his way out of a ticket. This time he decided to try the FOI technique I had just finished explaining to him. Never having spoken with the policeman before, he had no way of knowing what would make him feel important. Then Frank thought of something . . . the cop's driving ability. Frank had seen him in the rearview mirror, manipulating through the heavy traffic to catch up with Frank's car.

"You're a powerhouse behind that wheel," Frank told the officer. "With your ability, you must catch an awful lot of speeders."

"I get my share," boasted the officer, reaching for his pad.

"Well, you've got to be a real asset to the police force, with the ability to drive like that. I'll bet most of the younger cops could learn a lot from you." ·

"That they could," the officer said, beginning to smile. "Why, some of these kids on the force are little more than hotrodders. They know how to drive fast, but they don't have the judgment and timing that I've developed over the years."

The conversation continued this way for a few minutes,

and Frank pretended not to notice as the officer put the pad back in his pocket. When all was said and done, Frank had received a mild lecture instead of a speeding ticket. And, he'd made a policeman as pleased as punch.

As I point out in the comprehensive handbook, *Control Dynamics for Mastery Over People*, Frank's praise of that policeman was sincere. It had to be, because the easiest thing in the world is to spot insincere flattery. On the other hand, one of the most powerful forces in the world is honest praise.

Now let's look at some of the other ways the FOI technique can cause others to do your bidding.

HOW TO GET ANYONE TO DO ALMOST ANYTHING FOR YOU

First, understand that human nature is such that a person will sacrifice almost anything if it increases his feeling of importance. Why, for example, do you think that so many mayors of villages and small cities are willing to work for less than $3,000 per year, and sometimes for no pay at all? Why are disc jockeys on thousands of small radio stations willing to work for minimum wage, or even less? You know the answer. On the other hand, municipal garbagemen and assembly line workers are constantly demanding more pay. They get little or no FOI in their jobs.

Here's the second thing you should know: regardless of how well their need for a feeling of importance is being met, human beings are constantly craving more importance. Like hunger, it is an appetite that continues throughout life.

Third, people who are successful at handling others know that the single most effective method is to:

1. Dangle a feeling of importance in front of the other person.
2. Arrange matters so that he can only achieve that FOI by doing what you want him to do.

In Frank's experience with the traffic cop, it was Frank's offer of self-esteem that spared him the speeding ticket. He had obviously struck something that the officer was proud of—his driving ability. The officer wanted to discuss this with Frank, and hear more praise for it. This wasn't likely to happen if he were writing out a traffic ticket, so he put the pad away.

Another way to dangle a feeling of importance in front of somebody is to give the person a good reputation to live up to. Then watch how the person bends over backwards to do just that!

Linda S. was the manager of a candy booth located in the lobby of a shopping mall. The business was owned by a dentist who rarely could be there in person, and who thus depended on Linda to supervise the booth and see that it was staffed at all hours while the mall was open. Because of this responsibility (and the extra hours required when part-timers called in sick at the last minute) the dentist paid Linda well.

Then the dentist's wife decided she wanted to become active in the business. Although Linda continued to work behind the counter, the owner's wife took over management and scheduling.

"Naturally, we're going to have to reduce your pay," the dentist told Linda. "You are working fewer hours and your responsibilities have been reduced considerably."

Linda argued with him about this, pointing out she had recently moved into a new apartment and depended on the salary she had been receiving. But the dentist maintained that the business could no longer afford to pay her the fifty dollars more per week that she was receiving.

Seeing she was getting nowhere, Linda applied the FOI technique.

"You have always been fair with me," she told her boss, "and I know you'll be fair with me now. In all the time I've worked for you, you've been kind and generous. I know whatever decision you make about my new salary will also be fair and generous."

With that, the conversation ended. When Linda got her next paycheck, she saw that her pay had been reduced by all of five dollars.

"We'd been talking about a fifty-dollar reduction," Linda notes, "and here, thanks to my using FOI, it was pared all the way down to five."

She had given her boss a reputation of fairness and generosity to live up to, and that is precisely what he did.

FEED THE "NEED" CRAVING AND GET WHAT YOU WANT

A craving that everyone shares is the deep desire to feel needed. People who know how to motivate others realize this, and they stimulate action by feeding that craving. You can do the same. A powerful way to get another person to do your bidding is to arrange it so that by doing what you want him to do, the other person gets a strong sense of being needed.

One of the most effective state legislators I know is Bob A., who repeatedly gets reelected, even though he belongs to the minority political party in his district. Voters cross party lines to cast ballots for Bob because he's built a tremendous volunteer organization to drum up support for him. How does he persuade the volunteers to work so hard on his behalf? He makes them feel truly needed.

"People feel futile when it comes to big government," Bob explains. "They think there's no way to fight city hall. Well, I give them a way. I let them know that the 'little guy' is big with me, and I'll fight for his rights in the legislature. But, in order to do that, I have to beat the odds in a district that is enveloped by the other party's political machine."

Bob beats the odds by enlisting the support of scores of volunteers. He obtains these volunteers, and keeps them working by letting each of them know individually how needed he or she is.

"I don't just thank them as a group. I keep notes on what each person is doing, and when I get that person alone, I tell him how important his efforts are to me and to our cause. In fact, I mention the person's work almost every time I see him. This way there's no doubt in his mind that he's needed. How else can you motivate people to do such mundane tasks as licking thousands of stamps and stuffing thousands of envelopes, or pounding the pavements to distribute literature?"

There may be other ways, but there are no better ways, and the voting record in Bob's supposedly hostile district can attest to that.

THROW OUT A CHALLENGE AND GET WHAT YOU WANT

You've seen it work with children, but have you ever tried it with an adult? The fact is that adults, as well as children, will work exceedingly hard to meet a challenge.

You've seen small children struggle mightily to lug an object much too big for them, just to prove they can do it. You may even have thrown out challenges to children in order to get them to do what you want.

"I'll bet you can't put your toys away in five minutes," you may have said, knowing full well that the child could and would.

This type of simple challenge will work repeatedly with young children, but it takes something more subtle when you're dealing with older children and adults. Here's the Mental Leverage method:

1. Pick an ability that you know the person is proud of.
2. Politely voice doubt that the person has enough of that particular ability to satisfactorily perform the task you want done.
3. Stand back and watch as the person does everything in his power to prove to you that he does, indeed, have the ability.

Randy R. sells forklifts and considers himself a good salesman with a good product, but over a period of many years, he'd had no success in his efforts to sell to one particular company.

"They used half a dozen forklifts in their warehouse, and their equipment was wearing out, but I couldn't get the manager to pay much attention to my sales efforts or look at the literature picturing our models," Randy says. "He kept telling me the company president liked the brand they already had, and would buy that brand when the time came to replace the present equipment. This is what I heard whenever I made one of my periodical calls at the plant."

Randy is an avid believer in self improvement and, from time to time, he takes home study courses. One of them happened to include some sections on Mental Leverage. Being a salesman, Randy was particularly interested in the part about dealing with other people.

"I decided to use it with the manager of the plant where I was having no sales success," he notes. "One thing I'd noticed about him over the years was that he was proud of his status. He boasted that he had considerable influence with the top bananas in his company."

So Randy threw out a challenge.

"Look," he told the plant manager, "you know my machines are a heck of a lot better than the brand you're using. You've told me why you're not buying them. The president is stuck on the other brand, and it would take a lot of persuading to get him to change. I have no hard feelings against you; it would take more influence than you've got to get the president to change his mind."

Now there was a challenge! Randy had hit the manager where it hurt: the amount of influence he had with the top brass. He knew this would force the manager to live up to his boasts and attempt to prove that he had the type of influence he claimed.

He did prove it. Randy got an order. Not a big one at first— it was for one machine. But his foot was in the door, and as other machines were needed, they were bought from him. That one instance of using Mental Leverage has resulted, over a period of several years, in more than $23,000 in added sales commissions for Randy. Throwing out a challenge has been one of the most profitable things he has ever done.

HOW TO GET PEOPLE TO IMPROVE OR INCREASE THEIR WORK

People will stop at almost nothing to prove their superiority. When you want someone to improve the work he is doing for you, or to increase the amount, let him know that you think his skill or performance is better than anybody else's. Then sit back and watch him go like wildfire, so that your opinion of his superiority will continue.

The president of a volunteer ambulance corps tells me that much of his success as a leader in the organization has been due to his ability to get other people to increase their work, and one of the most effective tools in his kit is the superiority technique.

"I used to think," says Harry S., "that once I got to be president of the ambulance corps, I could spend most of my time on such important matters as fund-raising and long-range planning. But, when I finally got to be president, I found that most of my time was spent doing work that other members were supposed to have done."

After a few months of this, Harry realized there was a limit to the time and strength he could contribute, and that the only way to get the organization to function properly was to convince a lot of other people to do their share, or even more.

"First, I tried badgering them," he recalls. "At a monthly meeting of the corps, I gave an impassioned speech about how everyone must pitch in. There were nods of agreement and even a few supporting comments—but no concrete results. After the meeting, things went on as they had been."

Finally, Harry switched to one-on-one talks with selected members.

"I decided to get individual pledges of help, and in getting people to do what I wanted, I used many of the techniques I had learned while reading *Control Dynamics for Mastery Over People.* One thing I learned in that book is the method that gets people who are already working for you to do even more."

Harry made a list of the people who were active in the organization, performing at least part of the work they were supposed to be doing. Then he played on their pride. He went to each of these people, pointed out the great work they were doing, and explained how the organization was counting on them. Typically, he'd say something like this:

"I don't know of another person in the organization who can do this type of work as well as you can. Our success depends on you. That's why I chose you to handle a special project for me."

The special project would, of course, involve additional work along the lines of what the person had already been doing. Harry concedes that it might not be the fairest thing in the world, to throw extra work on people who are already performing fairly well, but in a volunteer organization such as his, you take the labor from where you can get it.

"And, thanks to the fact that people will do all kinds of extra work to prove their superiority," Harry says, "I found one of the easiest ways to get our jobs done was to make busy people even busier, doing their utmost to prove they were as superior as I said they were."

FIVE WAYS TO COMMAND ACTION

You've seen examples of five different ways to command action from other people so that they will cheerfully do what you want. You've learned how to win your way by giving the other person:

1. Self-esteem
2. A reputation to live up to
3. A sense of being needed
4. A challenge to meet
5. Recognition of his or her superiority

What each of these methods does, of course, is give the other person a feeling of importance. Although I've listed five ways to impart FOI here, there are other methods you can develop on your own. The next time, and every time, you want to motivate somebody, think about what you can say that will give the person the extra importance he craves. You'll be more than amply rewarded.

HOW TO RESOLVE A DISAGREEMENT TO YOUR OWN BENEFIT

Getting people to perform for you is one thing, and winning arguments with them is quite another. Is there a method for winning arguments and resolving disagreements in your own favor? You bet there is.

Here is what the method is *not*:

* It is *not* forcing your will on the other person
* It is *not* telling the other person he is wrong
* It is *not* telling the other person to shut up and listen

* It is *not* stunning the other person with brilliant arguments.

* It is *not* seeking a ruling in your favor from higher authority

If it is not any of these things, then what is it? The secret of winning any argument and resolving any disagreement is to stop arguing. Instead of trying to get the other person to swallow your viewpoint, accept his viewpoint.

"Now wait a minute!" I can read your thoughts. "Sure, if I accept the other person's viewpoint, the disagreement has been resolved. But in the other person's favor, not mine."

Right, right, and wrong. True, the disagreement has been resolved. True, it has been resolved in the other person's favor. But it has also been resolved in your favor. Confused? Please read on.

Here's how Benjamin Franklin explained it: "The way to convince another is to state your case moderately and accurately. Then scratch your head, or shake it a little and say that is the way it seems to you, but that, of course, you may be mistaken about it. This causes your listener to receive what you have to say, and as likely as not, turn about and try to convince you of it, since you are in doubt. But if you go at him in a tone of positiveness and arrogance, you only make an opponent of him."

In other words, get the other person arguing *your* side of the case! When someone is in an argumentative mood, when he badly wants to prove you wrong, why not tap all that emotional energy? Instead of listening to him prove your position wrong, arrange it so that he proves you wrong when you doubt your own position.

Can you see what this accomplishes? Here's what happens when you take Ben Franklin's advice:

1. You state your viewpoint in a moderate manner.
2. Your lack of arrogance disarms the other person.
3. Your expression of doubt wipes out the other person's blind opposition to your viewpoint.
4. He now is much more willing to think about your position, since it's obvious that you're not trying to jam it down his throat.

5. Not only does he consider your viewpoint rationally, he begins to see the truth in it, arguing that your doubts are mistaken.

What you've done, in effect, is allow the other person to argue your side of the case, and then you've allowed him to win the argument. By permitting him to save face, your position has prevailed.

SKILLFUL PEOPLE-HANDLING

People who watch Gayle J. at work are amazed at how skillfully she deals with the news media. Gayle is a corporate public relations officer, and her job is to see that her company is dealt with fairly in the press and on radio and TV.

"One of my biggest difficulties used to be correcting the mistaken, anti-business impressions that many reporters walked in here with," Gayle says. "For some reason or other, most reporters assigned to cover this corporation (and other big firms too, I suppose) begin with a chip on their shoulder."

Gayle doesn't know for sure, but she thinks television dramas have had something to do with it. "The businessman is almost always portrayed as a villain on TV," she points out. "When children are brought up on year after year of this kind of TV fare, and then experience the anti-business climate that's present in so many colleges, it's little wonder that reporters come in here with false impressions and loaded questions."

As a public relations specialist, Gayle's job is to correct the mistaken impressions and persuade the reporters that her company is not the ogre they think it is.

"When a reporter asks questions about our company, I answer them as fairly and accurately as I can. When a line of questioning indicates that the reporter has some preconceived notions about the company that are false, I try to correct them. That's where the arguing could start, but I don't allow it to happen. I remember Benjamin Franklin's advice. I calmly state the facts that disprove the reporter's misconceptions. Then I explain that, while I believe everything I've said to be factual, there's always a chance that I'm mistaken, and I'd be happy to check into any contradictions the reporter might have."

By expressing an open-mindedness about her own position, Gayle begins to win the reporter's confidence; he immediately recognizes that she's not trying to put anything over on him. This causes the reporter to look more objectively at the facts Gayle has stated. The outcome is often a much more favorable news story, magazine article, or TV feature about Gayle's company than the reporter had set out to do.

Another outcome, as you might presume, has been in the form of career rewards for Gayle. Her reputation as a public relations expert became well known early in her career, and she was offered a succession of higher-paying jobs by various corporations. Her current position as corporate vice-president for public affairs with a huge food processing firm pays her more than $85,000 per year. That's pretty good for someone who, less than five years ago, was earning $12,000 in her first job.

MAKING YOUR OWN VIEWPOINT STAND OUT

Do you come up with good ideas only to have other people reject them? Does your boss shuffle your suggestions aside? How about your family and friends? Do they resent any helpful advice you try to give?

If your answer is yes to any of these questions, then you need to know the rule that helps you get your way in situations such as those mentioned above. It can be stated as simply as this:

Make the idea appear as if it originated with the other person.

This is a lot easier to do than you might suspect, even when you want a person to change his thinking completely. One method is to do as Thomas B. Reed did. The veteran Speaker of the House of Representatives would carefully listen to his fellow lawmakers voice their objections to pending legislation. When they were through, Reed would get up and announce that he was about to summarize what everyone had said. He then proceeded to voice his own position, and it generally prevailed.

Another way to make an idea appear as if it originated

with the other person is to praise him for having thought of it, whether he actually did or not. People in the office managed by Pete R. rave about him as a person and as a boss, despite the fact that he gets so much work out of them that his is the most productive division in the company. How does he do it?

"When I see somebody doing something in a slow or inefficient manner, I don't tell the person that he's doing it all wrong. That would only create resentment, and I'd never be able to get my people to pull hard for me. Instead, I get the person to come up with the idea for improvement as if it were his own brainchild."

When Pete wants an employee to use an improved method, he compliments the person on the quality of the work he's been doing, adding something like this:

"I haven't watched you work, but from your output I can tell you've started to use such and such a method . . . and I'm really impressed that you've initiated this on your own. Keep on doing it that way!"

Does the employee deny credit for the innovation? Never. He basks in the praise Pete has laid on him, and if you think he immediately adopts the method Pete credited him with, you're right.

HOW TO IMPRESS PEOPLE WHO CAN HELP YOU

It takes only a sentence or two, yet it will be remembered throughout the entire life of the person to whom you say it. Every time that person thinks of you, it will be with a warm feeling. If that person happens to be in a position to help you, he'll sincerely want to do it.

The form these few words take is a compliment. The right kind of compliment is never forgotten by the recipient, nor is the person who expressed it. Fortunes, friendships, even marriages, have been born out of a simple compliment.

But not just any compliment will do. That's where Mental Leverage comes in. Anybody can pay a compliment, but it takes a bit of special skill to pay the kind that will have full impact on its mark. For example, here are some types of compliment that usually *don't* work:

* Praising an accomplished person for the skills every-
  one already knows he has
* Praising a person for qualities he knows he doesn't have
* Overstating your praise by gushing

If you were to tell a motion picture actress how much you
enjoy her acting, or how beautiful she is, she would naturally
be pleased. But the compliment would probably not be remembered for very long because it's the type that movie stars often
hear. On the other hand, if you were to have noticed, say, a
painting she had done and praised her for it, chances are you
and your compliment would remain with her. Of all the compliments Arturo Toscanini received following a particular concert,
the one he remembered most was from the lady who told him
not how well he had conducted (he knew that), but how good-
looking he was!

Eric J. earned a $20,000 bonus because he knows the
value of complimenting people. Eric works for a major cable
television company that has franchises in many communities.

"I was sent in to one particular community," Eric recalls,
"because we were about to lose our franchise there. The local
manager had let the quality of service slip, and residents were
pressuring the town board to give the cable TV franchise to a
competing firm. I could see that the first thing I had to do was
to get our most vocal critics switched over to our side.

"So, one by one, I called on every customer who had filed
a complaint. And do you know the first thing I did before
knocking on the door? I looked around for some attractive
feature of the yard or house that the owner would obviously be
proud of. It might be the well-kept lawn. Or maybe a sports car
parked in the driveway, or an attractive porte-cochère at the
side of the house.

"I'd tell the resident: 'The people at our office told me I'd
have no trouble finding your home because it's the one with
the beautiful . . .' and then I'd name whatever it was that I had
spotted. This would get us off to a good start. The fact that the
cable TV people had noticed something the customer was
proud of would naturally put the customer in a better mood to
listen to the word I was bringing—that as the new local manager, I would bring a substantial improvement to the service."

The upshot is that Eric saved the franchise. When the

town board conducted a public hearing on the matter, the original complainers failed to appear. Any skilled manager could have gone in to that town and improved service, but it took a special human relations knack to win back the trust of the people before the franchise could be cancelled. Eric's knack for paying the right kind of compliment had helped save a valuable operation for his company, and in return for that, he received the $20,000 bonus.

"That was five years ago," Eric points out, "and even though I have since been promoted to a larger franchise area, I occasionally have reason to stop by our office in that town. Customers who walk in to pay their bills see me and give a cheerful greeting. Many of them remember me as the man who was so impressed with their home. It's proved to me that such compliments are never forgotten."

A HABIT THAT CAN BRING UNEXPECTED BENEFITS

Eric would be the last person to say you should pay compliments only when you want or expect something specific in return. Get into the habit of looking for the praiseworthy in everyone you meet, and then don't hesitate to express that praise. In most cases, your only immediate benefit will be the pleasure you've earned in pleasing another person. But the lifetime impression you've made on that person can also come back to you in an unexpected form at the most unexpected time.

The compliment you've paid somebody a week ago, a month ago, or a decade ago could conceivably be responsible for some fabulous change in your life. The many people you've complimented will naturally think often of what you said, and one of them may think of you when the company he now heads needs someone of your talents to head a new division. Experiences such as this have happened many times, and they will happen to you in direct proportion to how often you sow the seed.

This is a book about leverage, and what greater leverage is there than reaping giant rewards from a simple compliment? The time to start sowing is now.

How to Use
the Written Word
to Get What You Want

Anybody who can read and write knows how to put a sentence together so that it makes sense. Unfortunately, most people don't know how to put a sentence together so that it accomplishes very much. They can't make it get them what they want.

True, if you write a letter ordering a mail-order product, you'll probably get what you want, but only because you're paying for the merchandise. A boss who sends an angry memo to his employees will also get what he wants, but only because the employees are afraid of being fired. What happens, though, when you don't combine your words with money or a threat? Are the words themselves powerful enough to inspire immediate action? Will most people even take the trouble to read them?

Mental Leverage shows how to get more results from every word and sentence that you put on paper. In this chapter, you'll learn how to turn out:

* High-powered words that generate interest and action
* Powerful letters that achieve their goal
* Effective memos that get people to move
* Impressive reports that score big points for you
* Outstanding résumés that excite employers

189

You're going to prove the truth in what Joseph Conrad observed: "He who wants to persuade should put his trust, not in the right argument, but in the right word." Thanks to Mental Leverage, you'll find that using the right word is actually easier than using the wrong one.

HIGH-POWERED WORDS THAT GENERATE INTEREST AND ACTION

In case you're worried about it, you won't have to increase your vocabulary. There are no word lists to study, no big and fancy expressions to learn. You already know all the high-powered words you'll ever need. The trouble is that you probably haven't been using them in the best way. Let's look at an example of what happens when you do.

There is probably no clearer proof of how well certain words are performing than in newspaper classified ads. The proof lies in the response you get from the ad. The responses from real estate broker Clint M.'s classified advertising doubled once he began using high-powered words (HPW's).

As Clint explains it, "People reading the classified columns have a lot of little ads to wade through. I specialize in apartment rentals, and with scores of apartments listed by various brokers every day, the reader can't possibly respond to them all. Naturally, he'll answer the ones that appeal to him the most. My problem was how to make my ads more appealing than all the others."

Clint didn't solve his problem. His wife did. Wendy heard about HPW's in a communications course she was taking, and she began using them in ads she rewrote for Clint.

"The results were almost immediate," Clint recalls. "The number of inquiries continued rising until it reached a plateau at least double the old level. The ads are no longer than they were before, and they're not run any more often. The only difference is Wendy's high-powered wording."

If you examine a column or two of rental ads, you'll see that most of the insertions are alike. They list the location, the number of bedrooms and bathrooms, and probably the price. Some contain a trite opening word or two in capital letters, aimed at catching the reader's attention. It would appear that most apartments are either *charming* or *spacious*.

Clint's original ads were no different. "I followed the format," he explains. "It's what apartment advertisers had always done."

But Wendy had a different idea. Sure, list the number of bedrooms and bathrooms because that's important, but lead off with a REAL eye-catcher. "I figured apartments could be more than merely charming or spacious. I picked a genuinely appealing feature of each apartment and made that our headline, even if it wasn't the type of thing usually listed in real estate ads. After all, the ads were being written for potential tenants, not for other real estate people."

Here are some of the headlines Wendy wrote:

Safe Neighborhood.

Free Electricity.

Kids Welcome.

Friendly Neighbors.

Watch the Ships Come In.

There isn't a fancy word in the bunch, yet these phrases are full of high-powered words. Because you probably find it hard to picture them as HPW's, let's examine just why they qualify. What you learn will help you in many ways, even if you never have to write a classified ad.

WHAT MAKES A HPW

If it isn't how big and impressive a word is that counts, then just what is it that makes it high-powered? First of all, let's define "high-powered."

> A high-powered word (or phrase) is one that gets people to
> do what you want them to do.

If you yell, "Fire!" in a movie theatre, people will scramble for safety. If you say, "I'll take it," to a sales clerk, the clerk will ring up the sale. If you tell your family that "dinner's ready" they will come to the table. In each case, you spoke words that brought the result you desired. To that extent, they are HPW's. But there's another requirement.

It doesn't take any special knowledge or ability to get action with phrases such as those included in the preceding paragraph. Anyone would know enough to use them in the appropriate circumstances, and the people to whom the words were spoken would be eager to respond. But what about situations that are not as clear-cut? The person who really knows how to use HPW's can generate the same kind of eager response in all kinds of situations.

Your HPW will get people to do what you want them to do when it meets three requirements. The word or phrase should be one that:

* Is easily pictured by the other person
* Relates to the person's personal experience
* Offers something the person wants

Let's see how Wendy met these requirements in the headlines she wrote for Clint's real estate ads.

* SAFE NEIGHBORHOOD. At a time when street crime is a serious problem in cities and even some smaller towns, a safe neighborhood can be easily pictured by the reader of the ad. It relates to his personal experience because he's thought or read about unsafe neighborhoods, and a safe neighborhood is obviously what the apartment renter wants.

* FREE ELECTRICITY. There's nothing hard to picture here. It relates to the experience of everyone who has ever had to pay an electricity bill, and it's obviously something a would-be renter would want.

* KIDS WELCOME. Families with children can easily picture an apartment where they are welcome; it's finding one that is difficult. This headline in a classified ad obviously relates to their experience and, just as obviously, it offers what they want.

* FRIENDLY NEIGHBORS. Admittedly, this is a highly unusual headline for a real estate ad. But Clint says the ad pulled a large number of responses, not just because the headline attracted attention, but also because an apartment building full of friendly people is easily pictured, it relates to the experience of everyone who has had (or even has not had) friendly neighbors, and it definitely offers something any renter would want.

* WATCH THE SHIPS COME IN. The headline could have
said NEAR THE HARBOR but Wendy knew that this was
more appealing because it offers something the reader
can instantly picture: sitting at the window and watching ships come and go. It relates to the personal experience of anyone who has visited a harbor, and it offers
something that many people would want.

"Fine," you say, "but I won't often be writing headlines.
How can high-powered words be of any help to me?"

Although you may not write many headlines, you will be
writing letters, memos, reports, and perhaps even job résumés.
Here's something you should know: HPW's are just as effective
in these things as they are in Wendy's and Clint's classified ads.
When what you write is easily pictured by other people, relates
to their personal experiences, and offers something they want,
you've got a winner.

By using HPW's, you are actually leveraging words. Here
are the reasons:

* You write fewer words
* You apply less effort
* Your writing has greater impact

Although HPW's are equally effective in letters, memos,
reports, and job résumés, the way they're used is different.
We'll look at how you can put a lot more power into whatever
you write.

POWERFUL LETTERS THAT ACHIEVE THEIR GOAL

"Writing letters has always been easy for me," Bart in-
sisted, "but I suspect my writing doesn't have as much impact
on people as it should. Can you help me?"

"Do me a favor," I said to Bart. "Please sit down at that
typewriter over there and write me a business letter. It should
be in the same style as any other business letter you write. Use
the letter to tell me what you've just told me in person—about
your desire to improve your letters."

My business colleague shrugged and then moved over to
the typewriter. Meanwhile, I jotted down what he had told me
verbally, as you see it in quotes above. A few minutes later, Bart

finished typing the "business letter" and handed it to me.
Here's how it went:

Dear Scott:

Please be advised that the writer of this letter has the
innate ability to compose written communications. What
is sought now is an optimization of said ability so that the
effectiveness of what is written is substantially increased.
Any assistance that can be provided in this regard would
be greatly appreciated.

Very sincerely yours,

Bart

Bart looked smug. "See what I mean?" he asked. "It was
no trouble at all for me to write that letter, and you've got to
agree that it's no worse than a thousand other business letters
that are written every day."

"I do agree," I told him. "And that's the problem. Like a
thousand other business letters, this one could have been
written in half the time, in a way that would have had more
impact on the reader. It would have been more readable and
more easily understood."

Bart was flabbergasted. "I don't know how I could have
written it any quicker," he protested. "And I composed the best
letter I know how."

"Yes, you could have written it quicker, and no, you didn't
compose the best letter you know how. Look at what I've
written on this piece of paper." Here's what I handed him:

Dear Scott:

Writing letters has always been easy for me, but I suspect
my writing doesn't have as much impact on people as it
should. Can you help me?

Sincerely,

Bart

"Isn't that much simpler and isn't it more easily understood?" I asked.

Bart had to admit that it was. "But," he said, "it's more like
conversation than writing."

"That's the point! Except for the greeting and closing, Bart, those are the exact words you used in speaking to me. They go just fine in a letter."

WRITING LETTERS THAT SPEAK

I glanced for a moment at the letter Bart had typed and then said to him, "Please be advised that the person with whom you are speaking has the innate ability to compose written communications. What is sought now is an optimization of said ability so that the effectiveness of what is written is substantially increased. Any assistance that can be provided in this regard would be greatly appreciated."

By the time I was through, Bart was laughing. "Boy, that sounds stuffy," he said. "In fact, it makes you sound like a pompous fool. And I think I'm beginning to get your point. You're saying that we shouldn't be any more stuffy in our correspondence than we are in our conversation."

Bart was indeed getting the point. The puffery that most people put into their business letters serves no useful purpose and is actually harmful. Letters are written that way for a variety of bad reasons:

1. People think that business writing must be pompous, coldly impersonal, and wordy because that's the way so many other people write them.

2. Business writers often try to cloud unpleasant information in a barrage of vague words, thinking such words somehow make it less unpleasant.

3. People mistakenly believe that stilted language makes them appear better educated and more capable.

Actually, in each case, just the opposite is true. You don't speak to people in formal, stuffy language, and you shouldn't write to them that way either. People who know how to write business letters that others eagerly read do it this way:

1. The letter is simple, warm, and as brief as possible.

2. Rather than trying to cloud unpleasant information in a barrage of vague words, good letter writers state it

matter-of-factly, and then find a way of emphasizing the positive.

3. Effective letters are written in everyday conversational language, and this shows off the writer as a clear thinker instead of a blowhard.

The next time you write a letter, and every time, ask yourself this question:

If I were speaking with this person instead of writing to him, what would I say and how would I say it?

You'll find this to be an easy guide for increasing the power and effectiveness of your letters. Then check each completed letter to see if its wording really does match what you would say in person. The secret of good business correspondence is writing letters that "speak."

APPLYING THE CONVERSATION TEST

When you ask yourself *what* you would say and *how* you would say it, if you were speaking your message instead of writing it in a business letter, you are applying the Conversation Test. You not only ask the question as you prepare to write the letter, you read over the completed letter with the same thought in mind.

My recommendations for applying the Conversation Test were included in a magazine feature on writing business letters, and one of the people who read that article was Larry D., who contacted me as I was preparing to write the chapter you're now reading.

"The concept of applying a Conversation Test impressed me so much," Larry reports, "that I decided to try it right away. In fact, the article gave me the idea of writing a letter to the board of directors of a yacht club where I had applied for membership a number of years ago. Because its harbor is small, the club has a long waiting list for new members, who are supposed to be accepted in the order in which they applied."

Larry had been informed at the start of the boating season that he was number 38 on the list, and they were only accepting about ten new members a year. About half-way through the season, Larry read the article on writing business letters and it prompted him to write to the club using the Conversation Test as a guide.

"I was really anxious to get into that club, so I told them that if some current member should happen to pull out in the middle of the season leaving an empty slip, I'd be happy to pay the full season rate to obtain that slip. I know that it's hard to fill slips half-way through the season."

Larry heard from the club a week later. They did indeed have a cancellation, and the slip would be his. Later, an officer of the club told him that it was the warmth and friendliness in his letter that had convinced the board to accept his suggestion. Larry's letter gave the impression that he'd be a fine club member. The mid-season circumstances allowed them to bypass the waiting list and jump directly to Larry.

GREAT ON-THE-JOB RESULTS

"That isn't the only proof I've had of the Conversation Test," Larry says. "I've also used it with great success in my job as a business supply salesman. I used to have to make a lot of cold calls trying to drum up new business. Now I precede each call with a conversational letter to the prospective client, explaining that I'll be stopping by on such-and-such a day. It serves as an ice-breaker, and my commissions prove that it works."

Of course, Larry is far from the first salesman to have tried using letters to ease the way during a sales call. But as one who has received hundreds of these letters over the years, I can tell you that few make a good impression. It has always amazed me that salespeople who know how to speak warmly and effectively with clients in person write cold and pompous letters that turn people off. Larry is a rare exception.

HOW CONVERSATIONAL SHOULD YOU GET?

Our everyday conversation contains some slang. Should our business letters contain it, too? Only to the extent that you would use slang when speaking with the person. Just because you use slang or poor English with the gang on the bowling team doesn't mean that you have license to use it in a letter to a business associate you barely know, regardless of the Conversation Test. The key is to keep your writing style as close as possible to the way you would speak to that same person.

What about special vocabularies? When speaking with people who work in the same field or who share the same hobby, we use special words dealing with the particular trade or hobby. I'm often asked if it's O.K. to use these words in the letters we write.

Sure, it's O.K., provided you know the person will understand them. Again, apply the Conversation Test. Would the recipient of the letter understand the special language if you were addressing him in person? Or did you include this language just to impress him? (If that's the case, eliminate the words.)

DON'T WRITE AT PEOPLE, "SPEAK" TO THEM

One of the best letter-writers I know is Clara L., who went to work in the administrative office of a large community hospital at a time when the hospital's relations with the community were not good. It wasn't just the skyrocketing rates that annoyed people, it was also the hospital's cold and impersonal dealings with the public that created problems.

"I decided that I'd do my bit to try to change that," Clara says. "My job in the office dealt mainly with discharged patients and their families who had complaints about bills, the care they were given, or the general conditions at the hospital. My function was to check into the complaint, then inform the person of the outcome."

The first thing Clara did when she took her job was to go over the file of letters that her predecessor had written.

"No wonder the hospital had poor relations in the community," Clara comments. "My predecessor wrote long letters spelling out, in detail, just why anyone who had complained was wrong. She listed rules and regulations to prove that the hospital was right, and she wrote in a stuffy manner that put the other person down."

Clara began doing just the opposite. She followed the

same guidelines for effective letter-writing that you've seen here. While I was preparing this chapter, she allowed me to examine the file of her replies to people who had complained. The typical letter contains:

* A warm expression of concern that the patient was not satisfied with his or her treatment at the hospital.
* The outcome of Clara's careful check into the complaint.
* A pledge to correct the problem (if the complaint was, indeed, justified)
* A "thank you" to the person for having taken the time to express his or her grievance, explaining that this keeps the hospital staff on its toes and helps it provide the best possible service.

"My predecessor was not a nasty person," Clara explains. "When people came in to voice their complaints personally, she was charming. But when she corresponded with people who had complained, her attitude was tougher, her language was stuffier, and the result was that people were even angrier than before."

On the other hand, Clara's letters read as if they are part of a conversation with the person, instead of something being written "at" him or her. They've paid off handsomely for both the hospital and Clara. The hospital is much more popular in the community, and Clara has been promoted to Deputy Administrator at a handsome increase in pay.

EFFECTIVE MEMOS THAT GET PEOPLE TO MOVE

Early in World War II, a White House aide wrote this memo about what should be done at government buildings during air raids:

Such preparations shall be made as will completely obscure all federal buildings occupied by the federal government during an air raid for any period of time from visibility by reason of internal or external illumination. Such obscuration may be obtained by blackout construction or by termination of illumination. This will, of course, require that in building areas in which production must continue during the blackout, construction must be provided so that internal illumination will continue. Other areas may be obscured by terminating the illumination.

President Franklin D. Roosevelt saw the memo and knew it was terrible. He rewrote it to read this way:

In buildings where you have to keep working, put something across the windows. In buildings where you can afford to let the work stop for a while, turn out the lights.

FDR's revision would have passed the Conversation Test with flying colors. He obviously knew that interoffice (or, in his case, interagency) memos should be written just as clearly and conversationally as mailed correspondence.

But an effective memo has to do more than pass the Conversation Test. That's because memos don't get the same respect that letters do. When you get a letter, you know the sender thought enough of it to pay first-class postage. On the other hand, nearly every office has a copying machine these days, so it's an easy matter to distribute memos throughout the organization. Nobody ever sends just *one* memo any more; copies go to nearly everyone. With every desk cluttered with so many memos, the one you write will have a lot of competition.

Here are two guidelines that will make your memos beat the competition. People will pay attention to them and you'll get the results you want.

1. Make a memo from you an uncommon occurrence. Dispatch memos only on subjects that are really important, and send copies only to the people who must receive them. A memo from you thus becomes almost an "event," and it will be read with interest.

2. Write the memo from the recipient's angle rather than your own. Demonstrate its importance to him, and the benefits he or his department will receive by doing what the memo requests.

George E. works in an office where there is a conglomeration of vice-presidents, department heads, division managers, and many others of memo-writing rank. And do they write memos.

"The paper work in this office alone must be enough to

keep the city incinerator working twenty-four hours a day, seven days a week," George muses. "When I was picked to direct a research project, I joined the crowd. Because I needed help from various departments, I began writing memos spelling out what I wanted. Funny thing, though. After the first couple of memos I wrote, they began to be ignored. People I'd speak to later couldn't even remember receiving any of the memos I'd sent them."

It was about then that George attended a seminar at which he learned the two guidelines for making memos stand out from the competition. Knowing there was nothing to lose and everything to gain, he began following them.

"I began writing memos only when it was necessary to put something in writing, such as detailed instructions, and I didn't distribute them willy-nilly. Copies went only to people who needed them. It wasn't long before people began to realize that a memo from me was important."

But George knew that even important memos are not always read. Frequently, people shove them aside with the thought of reading them later—and then they are forgotten. So he personalized each memo he wrote.

"I still do it to this day," George explains. "I've seen too many memos starting out with statements such as:

'I need your cooperation . . . ,'

'It has come to my attention . . . ,'

'I want . . . ,'

'My goal is to . . . ,'

Of course, no one really cares what you need, or what has come to your attention, or even what your goal is. All they care about is what is important to them. So every memo of mine begins with a 'you' angle: telling the person how he or his work will be affected by whatever the memo is about."

I won't say his memos alone are responsible for George's outstanding success in the company, but they have drawn favorable attention to him, and I'm sure they're a key factor every time he is promoted, something which happens to him quite often. In fact, George has received three promotions in the past year and a half, and he's the man to watch in that company. Nobody ever ignores his memos these days.

IMPRESSIVE REPORTS THAT SCORE BIG POINTS FOR YOU

People who have learned to enhance their performance with Mental Leverage find themselves looked to for advice and leadership. Their reputations as problem-solvers mean that other people seek their guidance in solving business, organizational, and community problems. That sometimes means writing a report.

ML people do well at writing reports. To begin with, they get the most possible mileage out of what they write because they use all of the techniques you've read about so far in this chapter. Let's review them. The reports contain:

* High-Powered Words that generate interest and action
* Conversational language that is clear and unstilted
* The "you" angle, demonstrating the subject's importance to the reader

Although good reports contain each of these things, they are different from letters and memos. For one thing, they are generally longer. They contain the writer's findings on a particular subject, and usually result from quite a bit of study.

Yet most reports go unread by the majority of people who receive them. It's a shame, because there's an easy way to make sure each and every report you write is carefully read by everyone for whom it's intended.

As the manager of a small branch bank, Phil H. wanted the local Chamber of Commerce to study the traffic flow problem in the downtown area to see if it could be improved.

"Since it was I who came up with the suggestion, guess who got picked to do the study," Phil laments. "But I was willing, and I began putting a lot of time into it. About halfway through the project, I wrote an interim report and distributed it to the Chamber members. I waited for their reaction. And waited. And waited some more, but there was no reaction at all. Apparently no one bothered to read the report."

Phil is not a quitter, so he continued his study. He was determined that, when it was time to prepare the final report, it would be written in such a way that everyone would read it.

They did. What was Phil's secret? What did he do the second time that he failed to do the first?

WHEN WORDS ARE BETTER THAN PICTURES

"Believe me, I thought of putting in pictures of bikini-clad bathing beauties," Phil says, "but then I decided on something better. After all, what do all people love even more than a sexy picture? The answer is themselves. What, other than bathing beauties, would get people to read the final report?"

No, Phil didn't include pictures of Chamber members in the report. (He wanted them to read the text, not merely look at the pictures.) However, what he did was to sprinkle their names in appropriate places throughout the text. Phil knows human nature well enough to realize that no person can ignore a report that refers to him personally. We humans also like to read about other people we know, and the liberal use of Chamber members' names added to the report's readability.

This one section of the report provides an example of what Phil did:

> The traffic light at the corner of Main and Division Streets in front of John Nolan's Stationery Store should be eliminated. Harry Nellis came up with the excellent idea of replacing the diagonal parking in that block with parallel parking to allow for a third traffic lane. Bill Smiley's store is located next to a vacant lot, and this might be converted to a mini-parking lot. The suggestion made by Marge Reilly, at a recent meeting, that the island in the middle of the intersection be eliminated is a good one, because it would speed up the flow of cars that now must circumvent the island.

If you were a member of that Chamber and knew the people involved, wouldn't that report be interesting to you, even if you didn't care one whit about traffic flow? If you thought it might contain your own name, wouldn't you read it carefully and hold on to it for a while? Of course you would. That's precisely what members of Phil's Chamber of Commerce did.

"I didn't have to wait at all for reactions to that report," Phil notes. "They all liked it. So much, unfortunately, that they picked me to conduct another study for them. Then, a year later, they made me an officer of the Chamber. Two years from now, I'm slated to be President."

It isn't being an officer of the Chamber of Commerce that pleases Phil so much, although he welcomes the honor. It's the fact that the top brass at the bank where he works have noted his growing prominence in the community. At a time when the bank is cutting back and laying off some personnel, Phil's future is assured. He recently became one of the few branch managers to achieve the rank of vice-president.

HOW TO MAKE A DULL REPORT HIGHLY READABLE

By their very nature, many reports contain dry material that hardly excites the reader. By making very few changes, however, they can make your next report much more readable. Simply work in the names of many of the people for whom the report is intended—the people you want to read it. Of course, you'll want it to appear as if there's a good reason for including each name. People's names can be worked in so they are a natural part of the report when you:

* Quote them
* Include suggestions they have made
* Point out how the information affects them
* Refer to related activities in which they've been involved
* Illustrate key points with personal anecdotes and experiences.

Include plenty of names whenever you want to leverage your word power in a business or organization report. Because people like to read about their friends as well as themselves, each name you include is a powerful magnet, motivating them to read the report from beginning to end.

OUTSTANDING RÉSUMÉS THAT EXCITE EMPLOYERS

Let's begin with the assumption that you're qualified for the job you are seeking. The problem is that a lot of other people are also qualified. You plan to mail in a résumé and a letter seeking a personal interview. Many other people will be doing the same thing. How do you get the employer excited enough about your prospects to grant you the interview?

A résumé is a résumé. It lists your personal background, training, experience, and qualifications, and that's it. There isn't much you can or should do to jazz it up. Is there, then, no way to make yours stand out favorably in a pile of résumés from people with similar or even greater qualifications?

There is such a way. But rather than dealing with the résumé, it concerns a letter that accompanies it. A résumé, as you know, is usually a reproduction, printed, photocopied, or mimeographed. On the other hand, the covering letter is an original, personally addressed to the prospective employer. There's where your opportunity lies.

Having opened and reviewed thousands of such letters, I can tell you that most people miss one of the greatest opportunities to impress an employer and virtually guarantee themselves an interview. Instead of making the one best move, they do one or more of the following:

* They try to be cute or funny
* They send a form letter
* They exaggerate their qualifications

If you want an employer to sit up and take notice when he receives a letter and résumé from you, if you want to impress him so much that he immediately wants an interview with you, then here's a rule that has a ninety-nine percent success record:

Include information in your letter demonstrating that you have taken the trouble to learn something about the company, are familiar with its work, and that, as a result of what you have learned, you are especially interested in working there.

Most people use the same wording in all the letters they send out, changing only the recipient's name and address. The letters give no indication that the writer knows anything at all about the company. Take it from one who has hired scores of people: when I receive a letter from that rare person who demonstrates a sufficient interest in my company to have learned something about it, and if the applicant tells me what he or she particularly likes about it, that letter gets placed in my "action" pile.

Most other people responsible for hiring feel the same way. The manager of a manufacturing facility and I were discussing this in his office the other day when he reached into his drawer and pulled out a letter to show me. This is the part he wanted me to read:

> I believe the recent award your company received for quality control was long overdue. So much shoddy merchandise is being foisted on the public these days that your reputation for quality products has always given people a warm feeling about the company. Your follow-up service is the envy of the industry, and I'm told you may soon be expanding the service department. I'm hoping there will soon be openings for experienced service supervisors.

"You can see from the date, Scott," my colleague said, "that the letter was written five years ago. You'd be right in assuming that the person got interviewed and hired."

"How'd he work out?" I asked.

"Fine," my colleague responded. "You're looking at him."

He handed me the second page of the letter and, sure enough, his signature was at the bottom. I started to comment about how remarkable it was that he had risen from service supervisor to plant manager in just five years. But then I realized that any person alert enough to write a letter like that had a lot on the ball.

Here's the moral: the next time you are in the job market, do a little research about the companies where you'd like to work. Then, when you write the letter that accompanies each résumé, tell the company in specific terms why you'd like to work there.

You won't have to wait long for a favorable response.

Outwitting Your Competitors

Most of the things you want in life are also wanted by other people. Sometimes there's plenty to go around, but in many cases there's fierce competition. For example, you may be challenged by others for:

* A job or promotion
* Cushy assignments
* A profitable sale to a hot prospect
* A date with a very attractive person
* Help from a busy person
* An exclusive contract
* Election to office

This chapter contains a set of easily learned maneuvers that help you come out as Number One in any challenge or competition. These techniques will blast through obstacles to give you what you want in life.

You'll discover:

* How to position yourself for easy victory
* The Backstairs Approach for climbing to the top
* The pawn-play that gives you a smashing triumph
* How to silence your critics and challengers

Every person has the ability to perform the maneuvers

you'll learn in this chapter, but Mental Leverage allows you to make the most of that ability. Applying these techniques, you should easily be able to outwit just about any competitor, constantly beating smart people at their own game and coming out with the prize you seek.

HOW TO POSITION YOURSELF FOR EASY VICTORY

"Whenever a lot of other people have wanted the same thing I wanted, I've just gone and taken it."

That's a highly successful man speaking, and an honest one. When he talks about "taking" something, Paul B. doesn't mean stealing. He means being the right person in the right place at the right time so that it's his for the asking.

Paul is now the president of his own international travel company, but for years he worked for various airlines. You may be surprised to learn that he started as a baggage handler at O'Hare Airport in Chicago.

"When I asked my boss about chances of being promoted to a better job, he snorted that baggage handlers are hired for their strong backs and weak minds and so I wouldn't qualify for anything better," Paul recalls.

But even then, Paul knew the importance of being in the right place at the right time. "And I knew that it isn't luck that gets you there. You put yourself there."

Today, it's known as positioning yourself for opportunity. That's precisely what Paul did.

"During my lunch and coffee breaks, and even sometimes after my shift ended, I used to go out front to the ticket desk. I got to know the people there pretty well, and they let me look over their shoulders. You'd be right in guessing that was the type of job I wanted next."

You'd be wrong, though, in guessing that one day a ticket agent suddenly became ill and asked Paul to take over. Such "lucky breaks" rarely occur, at least not that way. Most people who wait for opportunity are left waiting in the wings the rest of their lives.

No, Paul didn't wait to be asked. At the first opportunity, he stepped in.

"There was a crush of people on line," Paul explains,

"caused by some bad weather in the east. Hundreds of people had missed their connecting flights and now were trying to book seats on other planes. I walked up to the supervisor, who by now knew me pretty well, and volunteered to open up another counter position."

When the supervisor asked if Paul knew how to operate the computer terminal, Paul explained that he did, and the frustrated, overworked supervisor quickly accepted Paul's offer.

"I called the baggage foreman, told him I was needed up front, and stayed at that counter position for three hours," Paul reports. "When things quieted down and the supervisor began to thank me, I suggested that he put the thanks in writing—a memo to the personnel department suggesting that they consider me for the next ticket agent opening."

The grateful supervisor did just that, and Paul, as you probably have guessed, soon got the job he wanted. It was the second step in a career that saw him serve in a variety of positions with ever-increasing responsibility, until he was ready to start his own travel corporation. But let's get back to how Paul got that second job. If we review what he did, we'll see that four steps were involved.

THE FOUR POSITIONED STEPS

When Paul decided that he wanted to transfer to a ticket agent's position, these are the steps he took:

1. He learned how to do the job by becoming friendly with ticket agents, watching them work, and asking questions.

2. He made sure the shift supervisors noticed his initiative.

3. He patiently waited for an opportunity when there would be far too many passengers for the number of agents on hand.

4. He moved in to fill a need, and at the same time prove his ability to do the job he wanted.

Please note what Paul did *not* do:

1. He did *not* wait to be handed a job without any personal preparation.

2. He did *not* make a secret of the fact that he was learning valuable new skills.

3. He did *not* nag people to give him a new job when they had no logical reason to do so.

4. He did *not* make the mistake of telling the supervisors to call on him if they ever needed him; instead, he waited for the opportunity and then made his move.

There were any number of baggage handlers who, like Paul, had strong minds as well as strong backs, and who, like Paul, sought jobs of greater responsibility in the airline. Paul got the first opening, though, because he positioned himself for it.

The same Four Positioning Steps that Paul took will work for you. Here's how to beat your competitors and easily gain an opportunity you all are seeking:

> LEARN: Taking the initiative, learn whatever you need to know to handle the opportunity you are seeking.
>
> DEMONSTRATE: Without making a big show of it, demonstrate through quiet action that you are eager to learn new tasks and assume additional responsibilities.
>
> WATCH: Watch for an opportunity in which help is badly needed in your selected area.
>
> MOVE IN: Having positioned yourself perfectly for the opportunity, move in and prove you can handle it.

Paul credits positioning for many of the advances in his employment and business career. You've already seen how he used it to get his first white collar job. You can easily understand how similar positioning moves helped him climb the ladder quickly. But positioning also helped him establish and build his own business.

"Opportunity doesn't knock at your door unless you've paved the way," he contends. "But if you do pave the way, if you do set up the right conditions—it will knock at your door before most other people even know it exists. By positioning myself, I was able to find a top business opportunity at a rock bottom price, get preferential financing, obtain many lucrative accounts, win international travel contracts, and score as number one in many competitive ratings of travel service companies."

If Paul were to go back to the baggage handling area at O'Hare, where he worked less than ten years ago, he'd probably find some of his old buddies still working at the same job. For those who are happy with their work, that's fine. But there undoubtedly would be some (as there are in any job) with higher ambitions who have failed to position themselves to achieve those ambitions.

Positioning is not a magic formula. What it really amounts to is a turning of the tables. Instead of dreaming idly about opportunity coming to you, you plant yourself firmly in its way, so that it cannot possibly bypass you. The four positioning steps (Learning, Demonstrating, Watching, and Moving In) put you where the action is, ready and able to show your stuff.

THE BACKSTAIRS APPROACH FOR CLIMBING TO THE TOP

When I talk about climbing the success ladder, please don't get the idea that the ladder must be out front for all to see. Sometimes you can get to the top by taking a less obvious route. Let me explain what is called the Backstairs Approach. Here's how it works:

> While everyone else is competing for the most appealing job, you accept a job that the others don't want. Then you upgrade its importance in the organization.

In any organization, whether it's a place of employment or a volunteer group, there are always some tasks that no one else wants to do. These offer tremendous opportunities for leveraging a great deal of power and prestige for yourself.

The secret lies in the fact that when you take a job other people don't want, they're so happy you are doing it that they'll give you a lot of elbow room. You'll be free to make changes that give you a much more important role than anyone would have expected.

GRABBING OPPORTUNITIES OTHERS MISS

Three staff aides at a public library were waiting anxiously for the pending retirement of the librarian. Each of them wanted the job. They had their eyes so glued to that opportunity that a fourth staff member was the only one to spot an outstanding backstairs opportunity. A notice went out to employees one day asking for volunteers to visit each of the civic and community organizations in the city to explain the many things the three public libraries had to offer.

"No one else showed any interest in doing it," Jackie I. says. "They thought it was a waste of time because anyone who wanted to learn about the libraries could find out everything by merely stopping in. When I inquired about the number of volunteers, I was told there had been none. So I offered to take on the entire task by myself."

Jackie learned there were two reasons for the outreach effort. One, of course, was to attract more people to the libraries. The other was to get more community support for the library system so that it could expand its budget and programs.

Jackie spoke at the meetings of every organization to which she could get invitations, and she worked hard at building community support for the library system. She also offered to prepare a periodic newsletter that would be mailed to civic and governmental leaders and the news media.

"Before long, nearly all of my working time was being spent on this community relations effort," Jackie reports. "Not only was I appearing at public meetings, writing the newsletter, and preparing news releases for the press, but I also began scheduling special meetings of my own at each of the libraries, with the goal of attracting people who were not using the libraries."

Thus, Jackie took a task no one wanted and expanded it into a major staff position benefitting her employer (the library system) as well as herself.

"Although I had established a major staff position, it did not yet have a title or a specific place in the budget. That was the logical next step. The powers-that-be readily agreed to establish a permanent job classification to be known as Community Activities Coordinator."

True, Jackie did not become librarian at the branch library where she formerly worked; one of her colleagues got that when the vacancy opened up. But Jackie's new job is higher on the pay and prestige scale. Instead of being the boss at a branch library, she heads an important effort involving the entire library system.

"I found a job no one wanted," Jackie notes, "and made it into something big."

THE BACKSTAIRS ROUTE TO LEADERSHIP

The Backstairs Approach is equally effective in business, civic, fraternal, and volunteer organizations. For example, it's how Michael S. became state commander of a veterans' organization. Michael volunteered to head up a drive to establish a veterans' counseling service in the county where he lived.

"All the vets agreed it would be a good thing to have, but everyone was too busy to take the time required to lobby before the county Board of Supervisors and various community organizations," Michael recalls. "I was busy, too, what with my job and family responsibilities. But I knew I could spare an hour here and there to make the necessary contacts, so I offered to do it.

"And my efforts were successful. The county agreed to open a part-time counseling office in the courthouse. Suddenly I realized that if a counseling service was needed in my county, it was needed elsewhere as well. So I began visiting veterans' groups elsewhere, explaining how they, too, could line up governmental support. Several other counties eventually followed my county's lead. The various veterans' organizations were so impressed with what I had done that I was nominated state vice-commander. A year in that post was followed by election to my current position as commander."

The unusual part of it is that Michael is the first person ever elected to the top state office without first having served as a local post commander. He catapulted above scores of other people who, under normal circumstances, would have been far ahead of him in line for the state commander position. While they were waiting at the front door, Mike was climbing the backstairs.

WHY THE BACKSTAIRS APPROACH IS SO EFFECTIVE

This is a method that not only beats the competition, it eliminates it. Here's what happens when you take a job that others don't want and begin parlaying it into something much bigger and better for yourself:

* Others are so grateful you took it that they don't object when you expand the scope of the unpopular task.

* You introduce new procedures and techniques that increase your power and authority.

* Your work has now become so important that it is noticed by influential people.

* Either you convert the project you have created into a permanent position for yourself, or you use it as a springboard to something even more prestigious.

Jackie I., as you know, converted her project into a high-paying promotion for herself, while Michael S. used his project as a springboard that vaulted him into the state commander's office. I don't mean to compare either of them with P.T. Barnum, who was a showman more than anything else, but both of them have profited from something Barnum knew long ago.

"The greatest lesson I ever learned," the showman stated, "was that everything depended on getting people to think and talk and become curious and excited about you." What better way to accomplish that than by creating a position of importance for yourself and then doing a great job?

THE PAWN-PLAY THAT GIVES YOU A SMASHING TRIUMPH

In the game of chess, a pawn is sometimes sacrificed for the purpose of gaining an advantage over the other player. One contestant will move a pawn (or even a more important piece) into the line of action, tempting the other player to take it. It's done in such a way that, if the second player swallows the bait, he puts himself in a much more vulnerable position than he was before.

There are similar pawn-plays in real life, with one major difference: they are easier to execute. In chess, both players realize there is a contest and good players are always alert for the reasons behind a sacrifice. In real life, the pawn-play diverts your competitor's attention so that he or she doesn't guess what you're really after. This gives you plenty of leeway to move in and take it.

I first saw a real-life pawn-play when I was a junior in high school and had a crush on a certain girl we'll call Cindy. I finally got up enough nerve to ask her out, and we went to the movies and enjoyed ourselves. The junior prom was coming up, and Cindy let it be known that she wouldn't mind if I asked her to be my date.

At that time, Cindy was also dating another guy in school whose name was Fred. A couple of days after my movie date with Cindy, Fred called me on the phone.

"You know that record player of mine that you've been wanting to buy?" he asked. "Well, I've decided to sell it. You can have it for $75."

That was a bargain. Last time we'd talked, the price had been one hundred dollars—if it had been for sale, which it was not at that time. Hoping against hope that he wouldn't change his mind, I emptied the glass jar in my room, borrowed some more cash from my folks, and ran over to Fred's house with seventy-five dollars.

It wasn't until a week later that I realized why Fred had sold me the phonograph. He was gambling on the likelihood that spending seventy-five dollars would leave me too broke to ask Cindy to the prom. He was right. Later I was told that Fred and Cindy had a great time at the dance.

Fred had used a pawn-play on me. I jumped at the record player bait and this eliminated Fred's competition for taking Cindy to the prom. Since then, I've seen pawn-plays used in a variety of circumstances. I've used a few myself from time to time, and I've taught others how to apply this effective technique.

THE SECRET OF THE PAWN-PLAY

The purpose of sacrificing a pawn in chess, as in real life, is to get your competitor so engrossed in snapping up the pawn that he fails to see that the act of snapping it up will clear the way for you to move in and grab a much more important objective. Thus, the "pawn" you sacrifice to your competitor must meet these two requirements:

1. It should be something you feel sure your competitor wants.
2. His taking the pawn should make it difficult or impossible for him to obtain something that is much more valuable to you.

Irma R. met the two requirements when she beat out her principal challenger in the competition to win a color TV. The competition was being run by the fire department auxiliary to which they both belonged. It involved the sale of tickets to a fund-raising event that the auxiliary was sponsoring. The woman who sold the most tickets was to be awarded the color TV.

"With a week to go before the deadline, I found out there was only one woman who had sold more tickets than I had sold," Irma says. "Being that close to winning the prize, I had to figure out a way to beat her."

Irma threw out a pawn and her competitor lunged at it. Irma's husband is a painter, and the other auxiliary member had been after him to redecorate several rooms in her home. With a lot of customers seeking his services, he had put her name on the waiting list.

"I got my husband to alter the waiting list," Irma reports. "He put the woman at the top of the list. In fact, he called her to say he could begin work the next day if she wanted. She certainly wanted. The work took well over a week, and with her having to be there to help choose colors, etc., she had precious little time to sell any more tickets."

Irma, as you must have guessed, had plenty of time to sell more tickets. She easily surpassed the number her husband's customer had sold. The outcome: the other auxiliary member got her walls painted, and Irma got her color TV set.

Irma's competitor probably still doesn't realize that she was the victim of a pawn-play, and that's the way it should be. Although there's no way to prevent the loser from feeling disappointed that the prize went to you instead of him, there's no need to have him feel any bitterness toward you. The beauty of a well-executed pawn-play is that the other party rarely realizes that you engineered the whole thing.

A VARIETY OF PAWNS TO CHOOSE FROM

I know that you must be wondering if you'll have the right pawns to offer when the occasion arises. Unlike Irma, you probably won't be in a position to keep your competitor busy in a wall-painting project. There are, however, other things that you (or anyone) can do. Each and every one of us has a variety of pawns to play. As you'll see, they don't always have to involve a sacrifice. You don't always have to give something to win something.

Consider, for example, something known as the Diversionary Pawn. The dictionary lists one of the definitions of diversion as "a feint to draw off attention from the point of main attack." That's precisely what the Diversionary Pawn does. You play this pawn in either of two ways:

1. Keep your interest in the objective a secret. The other person, unaware of any competition, doesn't try as hard.

2. Divert the attention of your competitors by getting them interested in something else that, temporarily at least, appears equally enticing.

Now let's examine each of the Diversionary Pawns in action.

Diversionary Pawn 1. When word came down that a new manager was to be named in the discount store department where Todd V. worked, one other employee let it be known that he would go after the job.

"Boy, did he let it be known!" Todd comments. "He told all of us that he knew more about electronic goods than all the rest of us, and that the company would never make the mistake of promoting anyone but him to the manager's slot. He was really obnoxious about the way he said all this.

"The hard part, at least for me, was that he was probably right. He did know more about merchandising these products. But heck, I was an eager learner, and I felt my better attitude made up for any lack of knowledge I might have had at the moment."

Todd never let on to his competitor, or any of the other workers, that he, too, was interested in becoming department manager. He did, however, let the store manager know, and he made sure that his sales volume remained at a high level.

"I don't know if the other man ever bothered to apply for the department managership," Todd says. "He seemed to think it was automatically his, and he wasn't aware of any competition. Of course, it wasn't automatically anybody's."

No, not automatically. But Todd got the job. Part of the credit goes, of course, to his ability and hard work. Another part goes to his being smart enough to use a Diversionary Pawn so that his competitor wouldn't know there was a contest.

Diversionary Pawn 2. Florence V. and her husband go shopping for antiques at least once a month, but they face one problem.

"The only day Joe can get away is on Sunday," Florence explains, "and that's when a lot of other people are also browsing the shops. So, if we spot a particularly good buy, there's often someone right next to us who sees the same thing and tries to grab it before we can."

But Florence has her Diversionary Pawn ready. Loud enough for her "competitor" to hear, she makes this statement to her husband: "Joe, this item is almost as fine a piece as we saw next door. And that one was priced lower. Let's go back there when we leave here and snap it up."

A better piece next door, and at a lower price? Nine times out of ten the bait gets bitten.

"Even if the other person already has the item I want in his (or her) hands," Florence reports, "invariably he or she puts it back. After all, why buy that when the person can beat me to a better and cheaper item located just next door?"

What happens when the person fails to find the better-cheaper item next door?

"I suppose the person thinks that someone else got there first," Florence explains.

Although the diversionary lure used by Florence and Joe is imaginary, real lures are equally effective, if not more so. You don't have to invent a "better and cheaper item next door" in order to get your competitors off the track. You can use a real-life attraction. Consider these examples:

* When Margaret M.'s company posted an announcement that it was sending a team to Europe for a month-long project, Margaret arranged to be one of those picked to go. "They needed ten volunteers, but more than a dozen wanted to go. I told everyone that a good way to indicate interest would be to sign our names at the bottom of the bulletin board notice that announced the trip. Fourteen of us put our names there. The other thirteen thought that was all they had to do to be considered, but while they awaited the outcome, I sent a personal memo to the boss asking to be picked and reminding him of my qualifications. Naturally, I was one of the chosen ten."

* Computer salesman Calvin V. was manning a booth at a trade show when he noticed a banker he'd been calling on for months taking an interest in the system displayed by a competitor a couple of booths away. "I could see myself losing a sale I'd worked very hard to get. The only thing to do was to make the salespeople in the other booth too busy to spend much time with the prospect. At trade shows, ninety percent of the attendees are idle browsers, so I took a gamble and sent the next dozen people who stopped at my booth over to the competitor's booth. Then I walked over and began talking with the banker. While the harried staff there tried to deal with the rush of people, I eased the banker away to my own booth and clinched the sale."

* A best-selling author was visiting the creative writing class attended by Violet D., and the instructor said the author would have little time after class for personal consultations with the budding writers. "He had to go to the TV station for a guest interview, and then to the airport to leave for the next city on his tour. You can imagine how the other students fought to get in line to speak with him after class. I didn't bother. Instead, I quietly spoke to the instructor and volunteered to chauffeur the author to the TV station and the airport. She said it would be a big help. And it was, particularly to my own development as a writer. I got a lot of good advice during the hours I spent with the author that afternoon."

HOW TO SILENCE YOUR CRITICS AND CHALLENGERS

The average person is unaware of Mental Leverage and the techniques you are learning in this book. Thus when the average person is faced with serious competition from other people, he probably won't be able to call on the subtle, but totally honorable, methods outlined in this chapter for out-witting competitors. He may resort to far cruder methods.

Here are two of the things he might do:

* Try to demoralize you by forcing a face-to-face confrontation in which he verbally tears you apart, bit by bit.
* Criticize you behind your back so that others will think poorly of you.

Whether the criticism is done in person or when you're not around, you can't let it continue. But what can you do, short of wiring the other person's mouth shut? As you'll see, there are steps you can take that will be just as effective.

HOW TO GREET THE FACE-TO-FACE CRITIC

The next time somebody criticizes you unfairly, respond to the criticism with complete silence. Don't protest, don't defend yourself, and definitely don't reverberate with criticism of your own. Don't even allow yourself to get red in the face. Simply look at the person with as blank an expression as you can muster and watch him wind down.

Wind down he will. He expects you to retort angrily, and that might even be his purpose. He expects to be in the middle of a bitter confrontation, but it can't possibly develop if you ignore his thunder and refuse to play his game. For him, it will be one of the most frustrating experiences he's ever had. His words will fade to nothing, and the criticism will cease as abruptly as it began.

When Ernest A. began his office-cleaning business, he had to hustle for clients. Several competitors were active in the same town, and many of them competed for the same jobs.

"The owner of one office building," Ernie recalls, "somehow got his appointments mixed up so that a competitor and I were both supposed to see him at the same time, pitching for an exclusive cleaning contract. If you've ever tried to hype your own product or service while your competitor is watching, you know what a frustrating experience that can be."

It must have been particularly frustrating for Ernie's competitor, because while he and Ernie were waiting in the outer office to meet the prospect, he began blasting Ernie and Ernie's company.

"He really tore into me," Ernie says. "He warned me he was going to tell the prospect that I did sloppy work, that I overextended myself so much that I had to rush through most jobs, and that I was unable to hire capable people."

Through all of this Ernie did nothing except look his detractor squarely in the eye.

"I did put just the trace of a smile on my face," Ernie explains, "but other than that I showed no reaction. My competitor obviously didn't know what to make of it. I guess his goal was to get me flustered, and when that didn't happen, it was he who became flustered. He tried to continue, but began blabbering incoherently, and finally he just shut up."

When the prospect met with both of them, the competitor had not one word of criticism to voice against Ernie.

"Nor has he ever tried that stunt on me since," Ernie reports. "He knows that he'll get no response out of me. All the wind is taken out of his sails."

Speaking of sales, Ernie's firm got the exclusive cleaning contract for the new office building.

So here's the rule for dealing with a face-to-face critic:

> Don't respond to face-to-face criticism. Look at the other person attentively, but say nothing. The harder he tries to get you angered, the more he'll actually be frustrating himself.

If, as occasionally happens, the other person demands to know why you are not responding, simply ask him, "Would you?" Then smile, and revert to your silent treatment.

There is no way the tirade can continue. You have won by silencing your critic.

HOW TO SILENCE THE BEHIND-YOUR-BACK CRITIC

Obviously, when somebody criticizes you behind your back, you can't give him the silent treatment. But you can apply a variation of reverse psychology. Here's what you do:

> When word gets to you that a detractor has been talking about you behind your back, go to that person and praise him for the very same quality he has been criticizing in you.

Don't make any reference to his or her criticism of you. Be as sincere as you can in your praise of the other person. This is called the Equivalent-Praise Treatment. To illustrate, here's how you might handle various situations:

* If you are criticized for being a careless worker, tell the person how impressed you are with his own carefulness.

* If someone ridicules the way you dress, make a point of praising the person for the way he or she dresses.

* If you hear that somebody is telling people about a mistake you made, go to that person and praise the type of ability that keeps him from making the same mistake.

Chet D. had been picked by the nominating committee of his local civic association as the candidate for president. Chet had formerly served as treasurer of the organization, and the current treasurer was reminding members of an important mistake Chet had made while handling the group's funds.

"I had made a rather poor investment that lost a small amount of money," Chet explains, "and the current treasurer was questioning my ability to hold any kind of office. If I wanted to win the election, I had to silence him, so the next time I saw him I remarked about how fortunate the association was to have him as its treasurer. I noted that his judgment in investing our funds was excellent, and he could be proud of the work he was doing. Well, he beamed. He loved every word of it. And do you think he voiced any more criticism of me? Run down the man who had praised him so highly? Never!"

With his detractor silenced, Chet's election was assured.

"But what," you ask, "if a detractor keeps on detracting after you have praised him for the qualities he criticizes in you?"

In that rare instance, there is a follow-up step you can take. It's virtually fail-safe. Here it is:

> If a detractor continues to criticize you even after you have given him the Equivalent-Praise Treatment, go to him again. This time, repeat the praise, and ask him to help you develop the same quality you admire so much in him.

There's nothing a critic likes more than giving advice, particularly to the person he is so critical of. The mere fact that he has lambasted you proves he thinks he knows more about the subject than you. He's more than willing to tell you a thing or two, even when you ask him to do it in a helpful manner.

Do you know what happens? He abruptly halts his criticism. How can he publicly criticize somebody he is advising? That would be foolish.

High school coach Vincent T. heard about repeated criticism from a parent who thought Vince's tactics on the football field were wrong and would lead to a lot of losses for the team.

"Naturally, this made an impression on the kids who heard the parent's comments," Vince says, "and if I allowed it to continue, I stood the chance of losing the respect of my team."

The parent, Vince learned, was the coach of a Little League baseball team. The first thing Vince did was approach the man and praise him for his success with the ball team.

"But that apparently wasn't enough. A few days later, I heard about some more comments he had made. So I went to him again, only this time it was an 'I need your help' kind of conversation. I remarked about how successful he'd been in inspiring his team, and I asked for advice on working with my team. He gave it to me. And, after I thanked him, I said I'd be back from time to time for more guidance."

If you think Vince's critic was no longer a critic, you're right. In fact, Vince had won a strong supporter.

There are ways to silence critics, and now you know them. Start putting them into motion at the very first opportunity. I think you'll be pleased at your ability to leverage a bad situation into one that is clearly in your favor.

Equip Your Mind
for Super-Performance

When there's no time to ponder and there's no room for error, you've got to be good at making snap judgments. This chapter reveals how to equip your mind for super-performance when instant decisions must be made.

MAKE SNAP JUDGMENTS SEEM LIKE STROKES OF GENIUS

We're talking here about one-shot opportunities where you *must* make the right decision the first time and do it quickly, in situations where you won't have a chance to correct any mistakes. Some people call the ability to succeed in this type of circumstance "thinking on your feet"; others call it "crisis conduct," and still others dub it "performing under fire." Regardless of what it is called, it requires a super-performance that can easily be achieved by those who apply Mental Leverage.

The fact that you or anyone can perform brilliantly is proven by the people you will meet in this chapter, such as:

* The unassuming housewife who went on television and outwitted an educator
* The job applicant who got hired after outperforming people with far more training

* The salesman who closed a million-dollar deal with a client who didn't want to see him
* The man with a dream who built a prosperous business in a field he knew little about
* The meek individual who wowed the audience with a speech he had been afraid to give

What is the secret of these people's performance? It can be defined in one word: simulation. It puts you in shape for super-performance when every thought and every move count. With something as simple as a pile of file cards, you simulate crisis conditions you are going to face, and you learn how to beat them.

HOW SIMULATION TECHNIQUES TEACH YOU SUPER-PERFORMANCE

Two people who depend on simulation are father-and-son neighbors of mine. The father works as a control room operator in a nuclear power plant, while his son is on the high school basketball team.

When I was given a tour of the nuclear plant recently, I saw not one control room, but two. They were identical in every respect except that one really operated the plant and the other was a mockup control room used for training. The training room had all the same dials and gauges, the identical switches, and even the same sounds. Behind the scenes was a computer that created the realism.

"We throw all kinds of problems at our operators here," I was told, "ranging from a minor malfunction all the way to a potential meltdown. Our operators learn here, where no harm can be done, how to deal with every kind of situation. Then they're ready, when and if the real thing happens."

The day I visited the nuclear plant, I saw my neighbor on duty in the simulated control room. It was natural to wonder what a man with half a dozen years of control room experience was doing there. The answer was that all operators use the simulator periodically for refresher training and testing.

On the way home that day, I drove past my neighbor's house and noticed his son in the driveway with a basketball, shooting at the basket located above the garage door. The boy was alone, but his motions were as if he was facing a hostile squad that tried to keep him from scoring the winning point of a game. He wasn't just shooting at the basket, he was feinting, pivoting, and going through all the motions you might see a player go through when there are ten men on the court.

It struck me that Ricky and his father were both doing the same thing. They were using simulation to prepare them for quick thinking and quick action when mistakes would be expensive.

Ricky's father was using complicated electronic gear that cost millions of dollars; Ricky was using equipment that cost well under $100. Each was learning how to perform under fire by faking the fire.

ADVANTAGES OF SIMULATION TECHNIQUES

In a sense, Ricky and his father were both "shooting baskets," and it was helping each to become a super-performer in his own field. They both realized that simulation is a great help whenever you want to:

* Learn privately and at your own convenience
* Avoid tying up equipment that is needed to perform real work
* Prepare for a one-shot opportunity that must be done right
* Practice for a real-life crisis with real-life consequences
* Use repetition to strengthen your automatic responses
* Correct potential mistakes before they occur
* Be ready to walk through a new experience as if it were old hat

Another advantage is that you can simulate tougher conditions than are likely to occur in real life. This makes you more than ready for whatever comes. Chances of a major leak at a nuclear power plant are less than one in a billion but, because of simulation, Ricky's father is able to deal with that kind of condition whenever he wants, and he's ready should it ever occur.

You don't need to be a nuclear power plant operator or even a basketball player to benefit from simulation. This chapter shows how it can be used to leverage your mind-power for everyday feats that make you a better performer on the job, in your hobbies, in dealings with other people, and in nearly any pursuit you choose to undertake.

HOW INEXPENSIVE REALISM PAYS OFF

The first thing that most people who use simulation learn is that it usually doesn't take much effort or money to create the realism they need. As Barbara H. proved, it can be as basic as a pile of three-by-five-inch file cards available in any stationery store.

Barbara wrote a letter to the local newspaper protesting the planned closing of a nearby elementary school. The school administration had decided to shut down the building because of declining enrollment in the district.

"Enrollment isn't down very much in the school they want to close," Barbara wrote. "It's down in several other schools, yet it's this one that's being picked on. We are being unfairly penalized, and our children will now have to be bused across town needlessly."

The day after Barbara's letter appeared in the paper, she received a phone call from the local TV station, inviting her to appear in a joint interview with the school superintendent to discuss the controversy.

"They called it a discussion, but I knew it was really going to be a debate, and if you think the thought of it floored me, you're right," Barbara admits. "Who, me, debating the school superintendent? I'm just a quiet, uneducated housewife. But then I realized that somebody had to carry the fight against closing the school, or they'd just go ahead and do it. So I agreed to appear."

You'd be right in presuming that Barbara's experience is being related here because she used simulation to prepare for the debate. Naturally, she didn't have the means to create a mockup TV studio, and there was no need to. What she needed was practice in stating her opinions effectively and being able to refute any argument that the school official might put forth.

"The school district had distributed a circular on the reasons for the closing. I took that to my desk, along with some newspaper clippings containing quotes by the superintendent. I put each argument the school people had made on a separate file card. I even thought up some additional arguments they might want to use."

At a time when no one was home to interrupt her, Barbara sat on the living room sofa, shuffled the cards, and put them face down on the coffee table in front of her. She turned over the top card and read it. Acting as if the statement on the card had just been made by the school superintendent, she responded with an opposing argument. One by one, she went through the pile of cards in this manner, responding out loud.

On each of the next several days, Barbara repeated the process.

"I got so that I had winning answers to all the arguments the school superintendent was likely to make. This practice prepared me to come up with an instant and completely logical response."

Barbara did, indeed, have the right answers when it came time to do the actual telecast. After all, she'd been through it all before—several times.

"I hardly had to think," she says. "Whatever he said, I had an answer for, and some compelling arguments of my own, too. That television program drew a lot of response from the public, and it resulted in a big turnout at the next school board meeting to protest the closing. The board backed down, and the school is being kept open."

MORE VALUABLE THAN REAL-LIFE EXPERIENCE

One of the greatest benefits of simulation is that you can concentrate on your weak points without wasting time on your strong points. Barbara knew, for example, that she would have no trouble voicing her own arguments in favor of keeping the school open. Her weak point—the area where she needed practice—was in having quick replies to anything her opponent was likely to say. The flash card system provided that practice.

It's a lot like the flight simulator used to train airline pilots. If a pilot's weak point is, say, take-offs, he can simulate take-offs repeatedly, without having to land the aircraft each time. Or, it's like the electronic chess games that are so popular these days. They allow you to set up specific problems. You don't have to play through a lengthy game to get practice in the kind of situation with which you need more experience.

YOU CAN SIMULATE NEARLY ANYTHING

As Barbara's preparation for the TV debate demonstrated, you don't need fancy equipment to create an effective simulation. Barbara did not have to set up a mock TV studio. She didn't need a camera, lights, or even someone to debate with. All she needed was a series of arguments thrown at her in random order so she would not know what was coming next.

Thus, you can easily create a simulation to train for super-performance by remembering this rule:

> The only thing that has to be realistic about a simulation is the series of challenges that are thrown at you in unexpected order.

Barbara's flash cards provided the challenges and the only realism she needed. Similarly, my neighbor's son, Ricky, doesn't need a full-fledged basketball court to shoot baskets. All he needs is a basket, a ball, and his driveway. His challenges come from having to shoot the ball from a variety of distances and in a variety of simulated conditions.

Here are just a few of the challenges that you can easily simulate:

* INTERACTION WITH OTHER PEOPLE. If you've got to give a speech, make a sale, win a debate, or perform well in a job interview, you can't afford to flub. You won't flub if you prepare by simulating the parts that are toughest for you, making them easy when it's time to do the real thing.

* PROBLEM-SOLVING. One of the most common uses of simulation in the business world is to give executives practice in solving problems. There are various names for it such as Management Games, Operational Gaming, and Monte Carlo Simulation, but they all boil down to

recreating certain problems and having people solve them. As you'll see in this chapter, you can also benefit from simulated problem-solving in your spare time at home. You can use it to improve your performance in just about any mental activity.

* LEARNING. Everyone knows that the best way to learn something new is hands-on experience. What, though, if hands-on experience is impractical or too costly? Simulation to the rescue. It provides the same learning experience without the cost, risk, or preparation associated with the real thing.

DESKTOP SIMULATION

Now that desktop computers are common in business, one of their most effective uses is simulation. Executives set up business problems and then work at solving them, gaining knowledge and experience that might take years in the "real" world. The computers can easily be programmed to provide random problems for the user to deal with, simulating the unexpected challenges that crop up in business management.

As Barbara H. demonstrated, you don't need even a small desktop computer for that. Flash cards worked just as well for her as if a computer had been programmed to spit out random arguments by a make-believe school superintendent. On her own, she discovered something that cost a nationwide insurance company several thousand dollars to find out.

"But it saved us hundreds of thousands of dollars, too," Steve S. is quick to point out. Steve is the company's training director, and he had hired an expensive consultant firm to recommend computer systems that could be used in training.

"We're constantly entering new insurance fields with new kinds of exotic policies," Steve explains, "and people at each of our regional offices across the country need to learn the new material rapidly. They've got to be able to handle clients' questions and problems efficiently, or we'll lose business to our competitors."

Steve's original idea was to equip each regional office with one or more desktop computers programmed to give the local personnel experience in handling the new policies. It was going to cost just under $250,000 for fifty-eight computers and the required programming.

But then Steve read an article in a professional training magazine about flash card simulation and how it can feed out, at a fraction of the expense, the same type of random challenges.

Instead of buying computers and hiring someone to program them, Steve prepares a series of flash cards for each new type of insurance policy. On one side of each card is a question or problem dealing with the policy. On the other side is the solution. Prior to a simulation session, the cards are shuffled. Then, the user picks them up, one by one, and is presented with a problem to solve or question to answer.

"The computers would not have been able to accomplish anything more than these flash cards can," Steve boasts, "and our personnel find them easy and fun to use. They've even made it into a sort of game, scoring themselves on the number of correct answers. The bottom line is that I've saved $247,565, and achieved the same, if not better, results."

BUILD PERSONAL SKILLS WITH SIMULATION

You've seen, however, that simulation with flash cards is not just for business. It's a great boost in developing a variety of personal skills. The cards are used to simulate a series of events. Each event is written on a separate card, then the pile is shuffled to provide a random order. Barbara did this in preparing for her TV debate. The "events" she simulated were the arguments that were likely to be expressed by her opponent.

Taking one card after another from the top of the pile, you obtain a series of challenges to deal with, never knowing what will come next. Responding to one event after another, just as in real life, you quicken your mental reflexes and gain valuable experience.

Here's the step-by-step procedure for setting up your own simulation:

1. Buy a set of three-by-five cards in a stationery or variety store.

2. Listing one item per card, write out a series of ques-

tions, problems, or events dealing with the skill you are practicing.

3. Shuffle the cards.
4. Working from the top of the deck, practice with each card by answering the question, solving the problem, or deciding how to deal with the event.
5. Save the cards and repeat Steps Three and Four every time you want more practice.

People who use this system to develop personal skills report that its simplicity and its game-like nature are deceiving. It brings solid and practical results. But, I must admit there is a little more to it than has met your eye so far. There are good and some not-so-good ways of preparing and using the flash cards. How you do it can spell the difference between average performance and super-performance.

WHY AND WHEN YOU SHOULD CONDITION YOUR MIND FOR SUPER-PERFORMANCE

People who have never tried preparing and using their own flash cards sometimes hesitate to do it because they think it's not worth the trouble, and sometimes they're right. It's not worth the trouble unless the system is used to condition yourself for skills that are vitally important to you. Please consider these facts:

* Joggers run because building their health and stamina is vitally important to them
* Weight-lifters lift because building strong bodies is vitally important to them
* Student pilots practice take-offs and landings because flying safely is vitally important to them
* Boxers train because building their skill and stamina is vitally important to them
* Musicians practice because developing and maintaining their musical ability is vitally important to them
* Actors rehearse because putting on a good performance is vitally important to them

   * Professional golfers practice because scoring well is vitally important to them

Thus, if developing a particular mental skill is not as important to you as running is to a jogger or training is to a boxer, then you should forget about flash cards. However, if you sincerely want to condition your mind for a particular type of super-performance, then the flash card system will be worth much more than the effort.

For example, how important to you is getting the kind of job you've been dreaming about for years? Is it as important as, say, several sessions of running would be to a jogger?

That was the question I asked Lucy P. when she told me she wanted to become a newspaper reporter. Lucy had good writing skills but had never worked as a reporter except on school newspapers. There was an opening on the daily news-paper in her town, but word about it had been sent to the journalism schools and the opening had been listed in a trade magazine. Lucy would have a lot of competition from people with more training and experience.

"What do you think would impress the editor most?" I asked her.

She replied, "Being a lot more familiar with local govern-ment and political organizations than the other applicants. The paper is looking for a government and political reporter. But I've been away at college and haven't paid much attention to what's going on here."

When I told Lucy that in a few days she could become as familiar with local government and policies, even including the names of the people involved, as a longtime reporter would be, she found it hard to believe. I explained a special way this could be done with flash cards.

"Do you really think it's worth it?" she asked.

"How badly do you want the job?" I asked.

She decided it was worth it. She prepared the flash cards in the way I suggested and worked with them for several days prior to the job interview. The next week she called me to report she had beaten out the other applicants.

"The editor said he was frankly concerned about my lack of reporting experience," Lucy explained, "but he decided to hire me because the way I had answered his questions proved that I had a 'working familiarity' with local government and politics. He said that fact was important in qualifying me for the job."

TWO WAYS TO TRAIN FOR SUPER MENTAL PERFORMANCE

Training for super mental performance is a lot like training for a race, a boxing match, or a weight-lifting contest. You use repetition to get yourself in shape for the real thing. You repeat the most challenging aspects of the skill until they become second nature to you. The only difference is that, in this case, the challenges are mental.

Mental challenges are recreated in either of two ways. The first method deals with information. The second involves problems. There's a flash card for each of the two categories.

* QUIZ CARDS: These are used for information training. The information you need to work with is prepared in quiz format, with one question per card. The question is written on one side and the correct answer on the other. Lucy used this method to train with the civic data she needed to land her job. She took a local civic directory and transferred the important data onto cards, one item per card.

* PROBLEM CARDS: These are used when you are training for situations in which you will have to face a variety of problems. You'll recall that the problems Barbara worked with were the arguments that were likely to be voiced by her TV debate opponent. She listed the arguments on individual cards and then practiced responding to them. As you'll see, you can train effectively with a great variety of problems using this method.

The power of the flash card system is explained by what I call the Three R's of Super-Performance Training. These three factors train your reflexes to make brilliant snap judgments and to tap a wealth of important information. Your mental training has you:

* REPRODUCE carefully selected challenges to work with

* RANDOMIZE the challenges so they come at you in surprise order
* RESPOND to the challenges as quickly as you can.

By carefully selecting the challenges you *reproduce* on the flash cards, you greatly enhance the training effect. Your training time is concentrated on the specific challenges you need to work with, and only those challenges. Barbara needed to train only for answering the superintendent's arguments, and Lucy concentrated only on the local civic data she needed to know. Both of them were able to pinpoint their training efforts, and each quickly became an expert in the chosen area.

The cards are easily shuffled and this *randomizing* allows the challenges to come at you in totally unexpected order. You are prevented from memorizing by rote. Since there is no logical order, you deal with each item individually and learn it more thoroughly.

Drawing from the top of the deck and *responding* to one challenge after another, as quickly as you can, strengthens your mental reflexes. It prepares you for real-life situations in which the challenges do, indeed, come at you one after another. Just as a person who has trained for a race or boxing match is much more likely to win than a person who has not, flash card training for specific challenges makes you consistently more successful than your competitors.

HOW TO TRAIN WITH QUIZ CARDS

Quiz cards are great when you need to learn a lot of information fast and want all of it at the tip of your tongue, ready to be used at an instant's notice. You learn the information by:

1. Transferring it from reference material to the cards
2. Training with the shuffled cards

The reference material can be any book, directory, published article, or other source containing the information you need to know. The learning process begins as you locate the source material and write or type it on the cards. That gives you the start of a working familiarity with the data. Later, as you work with the cards, your knowledge of the data is built up to "reflex level," so that you can mentally retrieve any item at will.

Sid D. had a lot of learning to do when his employer, a major American book publisher, switched his assignment. A sales representative, Sid had sold business and professional books for years, and he knew the field well.

"Then, out of the blue, I was transferred to the educational book department," Sid says. "A company vice-president explained that there was a decline in book sales to schools and colleges, and they needed strong sales representatives in that department to get more business."

Sid had been both successful and comfortable in selling business books, but now he was facing an entirely new challenge. He's the type of salesman who doesn't like working just from a catalog of books—he wants to know a lot about each of the titles. This meant learning about scores of new books in an entirely different category. He also had to learn as much as he could about his new client field: educational institutions.

"The company threw me right into it, so I had to learn fast," Sid says. "One of the books I had been selling in the business and professional division explained the quiz card system for rapid learning, and this was a godsend to me."

To build familiarity with the new educational titles he was handling, Sid wrote the general topic of each book on the "question" side of a card, with the title written on the "answer" side of the card. Shuffling the cards before each use, he was presented with random challenges to identify books covering various topics.

"One of the big advantages of quiz cards was that I could use them almost anywhere, whenever I had a few minutes to spare. If I was early for an appointment, I'd sit in my car and use the time to do a bit of learning. I even used them during the commercial breaks while watching my favorite television shows."

Sid also created another set of quiz cards, this one dealing with his clients in the educational field. On one side of each card, he wrote the name of the particular school or college. On the other side, he wrote the name of his contact there and a bit of personal information about the contact.

"I had to get to know about these people right away," Sid explains, "and this was an effective way to do it. There was one particular client at the city school system who had bought very few books from us in the past. But when I called on him for the first time, he seemed impressed with my working knowledge of the books we handled. He placed a small order with me, and then placed succeedingly larger orders.

"So far, he's given me more than a million dollars worth of business, and recently he told me why. 'You always have the answers I need about the textbooks I'm interested in,' he said. 'You're not only familiar with the book, but also its price and availability. That's much more than can be said about the man who used to represent your company. Frankly, when you first called, I didn't want to see you. Now I'm mighty glad I did.'"

So, obviously, is Sid. He gives quiz cards much of the credit.

HOW TO TRAIN WITH PROBLEM CARDS

Problem cards put you to work with simulated situations, solving problems that you'll have to face in real life. Problem cards give you practical experience at a considerable savings in time, money, and perhaps even risk. Although you get your experience "on paper" where it is economical and safe, the experience can be amazingly close to the real thing.

When Gerry W. got out of the service, he used the pilot's training he'd received, his personal savings, and a bank loan to begin a helicopter service at the local airport. It was a business he'd dreamed about during his years in the military, but it wasn't making the money he'd hoped for. Not, that is, until he entered a phase of the business about which he knew next to nothing. Then things started to pick up.

Gerry accepted an offer to provide a traffic reporting service for a radio station, flying above the highways during morning and afternoon commuting periods and reporting on road conditions over the air.

"Of course, the flying part was no problem," Gerry notes, "but being able to describe traffic tie-ups quickly and understandably had me worried. I'm a pilot, not a radio announcer. But practicing with problem cards helped me become one fast."

HOW TO SET UP A MENTAL "LINK TRAINER"

Many student pilots gain valuable experience using flight simulators such as a Link Trainer. Gerry reasoned that if simulation works for flight training, it can also be effective in training for traffic reporting.

The procedure that Gerry followed in creating his problem cards and then working with them can be used to set up almost any type of simulation. Here are the steps:

1. Choose a variety of problems to simulate. Gerry was able to do this by monitoring other radio stations. He wrote down all of the traffic problems reported by their chopper pilots, listing one situation per card. He didn't write everything the reporter said, but simply listed the condition being reported, such as "Car stalled left lane Route 1 at Bay Street."

2. Create more problem cards than you'll need at one practice session, so that by shuffling them, you'll get a good random sampling each time. As you've learned, an important part of the practice comes from dealing rapidly with a succession of problems in unexpected order. One of the skills Gerry had to learn was memorizing five or six different situations and then reporting them all within one minute of air time. He would have to fly over a broad area, and then, in his next broadcast, report on everything significant he'd seen. He prepared enough problem cards to provide him with a large variety of situations with which to practice.

3. Using a shuffled deck, pick cards from the top of the pile and practice making the decisions or taking the actions required by each card. Gerry did this by grabbing a handful of cards, looking at them briefly, and then putting them aside while he voiced a simulated report telling about all of the conditions listed on the cards.

4. Build your problem-solving reflexes by working with the cards frequently. Keep at it until dealing with the situations becomes second nature and you can do it almost without thinking. Gerry had one-hour practice

sessions two or three times a day, and, by the end of the first week, he was handling his simulated traffic reports easily and smoothly. At one of his final practice sessions, he recorded his voice reports and the playback sounded totally professional.

To say the radio station was pleased with his performance from the very first day was an understatement. Not knowing that he had built up quite a bit of practical experience with the problem cards, the station management was amazed at how easily and well he did his reports. The traffic reports have been responsible for turning his business into an extremely profitable enterprise. Gerry recently bought a second helicopter and hired a pilot to handle some of the nonreporting workload.

SOLITAIRE GAME THEORY PREPARES YOU FOR THE TOUGHEST OPPONENT

"Game Theory" is what businesses use to train their executives to develop top money-making strategy. The executives are pitted against each other in simulated business situations, and they compete as if they were corporations battling one another. It's a game, but it's also tough, and it's designed to be a lot like business competition in the real world.

As you've seen in this chapter, individuals can profit greatly from game theory, too. In our case, the game is more like solitaire. Not always having other people to join in our training simulations, it's us against a deck of cards. But when done in the manner you've seen spelled out here, it has a powerful training effect. Depending on what you put on the cards, it can prepare you for any type of competition in real life, even the toughest of opponents.

You've seen, for example, how problem cards converted a housewife into an accomplished television debater, and a chopper pilot into a radio reporter, each in a week's time. Here, from my files, are some other examples of people who have been greatly helped by flash cards:

* A young man got a job as a city limousine driver without ever having driven the city streets, because flash cards gave him the needed practice with locations and addresses.

* A public relations man for a major oil company uses flash cards to simulate reporters' questions when he has to prepare for a news conference.

* A prison inmate who read about flash cards in a business book he got out of the library used the system to practice dealing with questions from the parole board; the practice paid off, because his answers pleased the board enough so that it granted him early parole.

* A woman who dreaded having to deal with foreign currency on a trip overseas made up flash cards to give her practice with the different values, and she was able to handle her trip with flying colors.

Finally there's the experience of Nick E., a friend of mine who practically fainted when his boss gave him the assignment of speaking before business and civic groups to push for the approval of a highway rebuilding project. It wasn't that Nick was afraid to appear before the public; the problem was his fear of sounding stupid.

"I'd never been able to express myself particularly well," Nick explains. "Even in friendly conversation, I got the feeling that people were losing interest soon after I started to talk."

But an assignment from one's boss is something that has to be done. Nick reasoned that the way to get people to pay attention to him was to be as brief as he could be in his introductory statements, and then open the floor to questions. It stood to reason that if people asked questions, they'd certainly be interested in the answers.

Did Nick have all the answers? Not at first. But some work with flash cards changed things. He made a list of all the controversial aspects of the highway proposal and listed one item per card. During practice sessions he'd pick a card at random and assume that the topic listed on the card had been asked him in the form of a question.Then he'd respond to the question.

"Shutting myself up in my room at night to practice, I was quickly able to build not only a deftness at answering the questions, but also the confidence I needed. And, after my first speaking engagement, my confidence really soared. There were several speakers that day, but people tell me my performance was by far the most impressive. You want to know something? It turned out to be a lot easier than my practice sessions!"

That, of course, is what simulation is all about. You've equipped your mind for super-performance so that when the real thing comes along, it's a breeze.

−14−

Leverage
Your Mental Power
with the
Knowledge of Others

Leverage, as you know, involves using a little of your own power to benefit from a lot of somebody else's. When you buy a product on time, your buying power is greatly expanded by that of the lender. Business and real estate fortunes are built by people who control vast empires with just a little of their own cash.

So far in this book, we've been discussing ways to leverage your brainpower so that your own mental abilities are expanded. But why not go the full leverage route and follow the same principle the installment buyers and fortune-builders apply? Why not use a little of your own intelligence to benefit from a vast array of other people's knowledge and intelligence?

HOW TO GET FREE ADVICE FROM EXPERTS

When Cyrus S. went into business for himself, he used more than one kind of leverage. By buying a franchise, he was able to open a $100,000 store with less than $25,000 down. The franchisor and the bank took care of the rest; that was the financial leverage he used. But Cy also applied leverage of the mental variety. He used the knowledge of others to help him pick the best available franchise.

It was Mental Leverage, in fact, that kept Cy from picking a bad franchise. He had practically settled on a particular firm that impressed him. It was a computer store franchise, and its advertising literature and the claims of its franchise sales manager almost convinced him that it was a great money-making opportunity.

But then Cy decided to do some field-checking. He went to see some of the owners of franchised stores in the chain, and they told him they were dissatisfied with what the parent company was doing for them—or doing to them, to be more accurate.

Next, Cy conferred with owners of other computer store franchises and found that one chain in particular was doing very well by its franchise owners. All of them were happy and prosperous. It was a firm that did little recruiting of new franchise owners, and Cy had hardly considered it during his initial search. This time, however, he followed through, and experience has proven that the advice he received from the franchise owners was excellent. Cy, too, is now a happy and prosperous owner of a computer store

YOU CAN PICK AMERICA'S BEST BRAINS

If you've never tried what I'm about to tell you, you're about to make an exciting discovery. You'll be pleasantly surprised to learn that:

Experts in every field—the people with the practical, working experience—are almost always happy to advise you and provide you with valuable information free of charge.

The trouble with Americans is that we're such do-it-yourselfers that we're afraid to ask for advice. We hesitate to seek help from the people with the inside track on what we want to know. When we do seek information and advice, we go to the wrong people. We tend to do either of the following:

* We go to highly paid consultants who overcharge
* We trust theorists in ivory towers who've had little or no practical experience

Why pay a consultant when you can get more accurate information and better advice free? Why trust the professors who may know all about the theory but can't hold a candle to the actual achievers? The real experts—those who are actively doing what we want to learn about—are almost always happy to help. The only exceptions are when helping you might cost them business or money.

It would be difficult, for example, to get a doctor to give you free medical advice. That would be giving away what it took him thousands of dollars and years of study to learn. On the other hand, I've received a lot of free advice from doctors . . . on the nonmedical subjects about which some of them happen to know a lot. A doctor helped me pick good investment land in Vermont, for example. It was no money out of his pocket, and he was proud of his real estate knowledge and more than willing to share it.

In the same vein, if Cy had visited computer store owners in the same city where he hoped to open one of his own, they would not have wanted to give him advice. Why encourage competition?

This leads us to Rule Number One for leveraging your mental power with the knowledge of others:

> Free information and advice is readily available from people who have nothing to lose by giving it to you.

Naturally, the help you seek doesn't have to be related to a business. You can get all the help you need in almost any field and, as you'll discover, it's yours for the asking.

WHY EXPERTS ARE ANXIOUS TO HELP YOU

Whether they'll admit it or not, experts are proud of their accomplishments. When a person has achieved a degree of knowledge or expertise well above the norm, he's proud of that fact and welcomes recognition for it. That's why most experts love to be asked for advice; it's an acknowledgment by others that they have superior knowledge.

Granted, nobody's going to give away trade secrets, but most of the knowledge you need to advance your career, business, or other special interest is not in the trade secret category. It's information that is readily available when you know where to look. The problem is that most people don't know where to look.

The mistake most people make is turning to professional experts instead of practical experts. Perhaps some definitions are in order:

* *Professional Expert:* One who has studied a field and is in the business of advising others about it.

* *Practical Expert:* One who works in a particular field, day in and day out, and whose knowledge has come from practical experience rather than, or in addition to, book learning.

This is not to say that you shouldn't go to a doctor when you're ill or a lawyer when somebody sues you. We're talking here about obtaining working knowledge that will help you pursue a special interest.

When people in the company where Ralph I. works need advice on buying a car, they usually don't check the road tests in the car and consumer magazines. Instead, they go to Ralph. They've learned that he can give them better advice about cars than they're likely to get anywhere else. His secret? It's simple: Ralph has a network of contacts in the car field—people who drive and maintain all kinds of domestic and foreign cars.

Whenever he needs information about a specific car, or real-life data on how well it performs (rather than brief field tests), he consults the people in his network. Ralph began building the network when the management in his company handed him the job of managing the firm's small fleet of cars.

"This involved arranging to keep them well maintained and replacing them when the need arose," Ralph explains. "All of a sudden I was given a job that required information I didn't have. I still don't have access to all the information I need, but I certainly know where to get it. And that's how I can help out the people who work with me when they need car-buying advice. My buddies on the 'network' can tell me just which car has the best mileage, handling ability, or repair record—whatever my friends or I need to know."

Because Ralph knows how to get firsthand information from others who are most likely to have it, he's been able to perform exceptionally well in his job and provide a valuable service to his friends. Much of the credit goes, naturally, to his knowledge network.

Let's see how a similar kind of knowledge network can also be of help to you.

ESTABLISH YOUR OWN KNOWLEDGE NETWORK

A Knowledge Network, a ready-reference list of people willing and able to tell you what you need to know, can bring big changes to your life. When you leverage your own knowledge with the know-how of the people on your network, you can:

* Set bigger goals for yourself
* Be told the best way to advance your career
* Keep on top of the best opportunities for switching careers
* Be armed with all the knowledge you need to make important decisions affecting the rest of your life
* Avoid making mistakes that many uninformed people are apt to make
* Know exactly where to turn for informative help when you need it

The first thing you must do, before you can get this kind of help, is to pinpoint the type of knowledge that can do the most for you. Do you need to know more about your line of work so that you can advance faster? Is there a new business field you'd like to explore? Or is there some special personal interest you wish to pursue in your spare time?

Once you have determined the kind of knowledge you want, you'll be surprised to discover how many people you already know who can provide some of that knowledge. Start your list with these names.

Charlie N. was a newspaper reporter with the unusual goal (for a reporter) of moving into newspaper management. The trouble was, he knew very little about business in general and newspaper management in particular.

"A reporter is aware more than anyone of the advantage of building a network of information sources," Charlie says, "but it wasn't until I sat down and started thinking about my career goals that I realized how such a network could help me personally. I don't mean contacts who could pull strings for me. I mean people who had information that could help me get qualified for managing a paper."

Charlie began making a network list that included the names of all the people he knew in the business office of his paper, and a couple of contacts on other papers in the area. Did these people know they were part of Charlie's Knowledge Network? Not at all. Rule Number Two for leveraging your mental power with the knowledge of others goes like this:

> The people you've selected for your network don't need to know that such a network even exists.

Charlie certainly didn't call up his friends and say "Congratulations, buddy, you've won a spot on the 'Help Charlie with Information' Network." What he did was think about how each of them might be able to help him with information. Then, whenever he encountered one of the network members, he would, in a seemingly casual manner, steer the conversation toward the knowledge he wanted.

Here are some of the things Charlie set out to learn from his network:

* How newspaper management personnel are recruited
* The qualifications sought by those who do the hiring
* Where the best opportunities exist
* Any specialized studies or training that might be required
* General salary ranges
* The newspaper chains that managers want most to work for
* Newspaper companies to avoid
* Names of other people to contact for additional information

By posing these questions of the appropriate people—people he already knew—Charlie was able to obtain inside information that would have been available in no other way. It helped him push his career in the new direction he was seeking.

Thanks to the solid information and guidance he got from the people on his network, Charlie did succeed in switching to management and, the last I heard from him, he was managing a daily paper in the midwest. It's part of one of America's great newspaper chains which, I am sure, has its eye on Charlie for even bigger and better management positions.

HOW TO EXPAND YOUR KNOWLEDGE NETWORK

Your knowledge network will grow as large as you want it to be. Rule Number Three for leveraging your mental power states:

Starting with people you know, your list can easily be expanded by obtaining additional names from people already on the list.

You'll recall that obtaining the names of additional contacts was one of Charlie's objectives. His network began with about a dozen names and quickly doubled in size, thanks to the additional names given by his friends.

When Marjorie G. decided that she wanted to start a home-based business selling imported jewelry items by direct mail, her knowledge of the mail-order business was next to nil.

"I read a few books on the subject," Marjorie explains, "and obtained some of the rudiments that way. But what I really needed was practical, inside knowledge on how to price the items, where to advertise, what to expect in the way of orders, and what direct-mail selling methods work best with (a) imported merchandise, and (b) jewelry."

Most people don't have a large circle of friends in the mail-order business, and Marjorie was no exception. Did she have to start from scratch in creating a Knowledge Network? Not at all. Here are some of the acquaintances included in her initial list:

* A jeweler
* The manager of a gift shop that also sells through the mail
* The director of the local Chamber of Commerce
* A copywriter for an advertising agency

"Four people didn't seem like much to start with," Marjorie concedes, "but that's all I could come up with. And do you know something? When I explained to each of them what I hoped to do and asked if they could recommend anyone else to consult, each of them gave me several names. Within a week my original list of four had grown to fourteen."

The jeweler knew of an importer, a mail-order specialist, and another jeweler who dealt in imported costume jewelry. The others had similar references in their own fields. Marjorie was quickly off and running with her Knowledge Network.

"Within a month, my contacts with these people had given me more inside information than reading a hundred books or attending dozens of seminars could possibly have provided," she boasts.

The advice she got must have been good. Her business was a quick hit, making a fine profit almost from the start. It has long since moved out of her home. Marjorie is the kingpin of a prosperous enterprise now located in a large converted factory building. It grosses well over a million dollars per year.

HOW TO GET HELP FROM PEOPLE YOU DON'T KNOW

At this point, you may have a question that is often asked me about the value of establishing a personal Knowledge Network. You may be wondering about how to obtain information from people you've never met.

While it's true that experts are almost always happy to provide the information you need if they have nothing to lose by giving it to you, how do you approach them in the first place? That's the question that's on many people's minds . . . and perhaps yours.

We get some answers from Victor D., who uses his Knowledge Network to learn all he can about American antiques. Unlike the other people you've met in this chapter so far, Vic did not establish the network to advance his career or business. He collects antiques as a hobby. Vic and his wife spend many weekends browsing through country shops and attending flea markets and auctions, constantly on the lookout for early Americana.

"But I still have a lot to learn," Vic admits. "After being

stuck a few times with items that were not worth nearly what I paid for them, I decided to get the best information and advice I could. Since impartial advice is certainly not going to come from someone who is trying to sell you something, I couldn't ask the antique dealers themselves for that type of information. What I could do and did was ask them to recommend experts I could contact about early Americana—other collectors perhaps more experienced than I."

The dealers willingly gave him names of people to contact, and Vic soon had the basis of a Knowledge Network, made up entirely of people he had never met. He used several different approaches in contacting them, but he found all of them helpful. Here are some of the approaches Vic finds especially effective:

1. Give the name of the person who referred you. Example: "John Smith at Countryside Antiques said you'd be able to answer a question I have."

2. Play to the person's pride. Example: "You are an expert on furniture from the American Federal period. Something about that furniture has been puzzling me and I'm sure you can explain it."

3. Make a straight-out appeal for help. Example: "I've started to collect early American furniture, but I'm afraid I don't yet know genuine from imitation. Perhaps you can advise me on a piece I saw the other day."

YOU CAN FORM A MUTUAL INTEREST NETWORK

It's time to revise Rule Number Two for leveraging your mental power with the knowledge of others. As you'll recall, the rule says the people you picked for your network don't need to know that such a network even exists.

The revision? Simply this:

Certain types of knowledge are best learned through a Mutual Interest Network, in which all participants actively share their knowledge and experience with each other.

A Mutual Interest Network (MIN) is much like the various hobby, professional, and special interest organizations that exist all over the country, except that it is not a formal organization. It has no officers, no dues to pay, no committees to serve on. It's just a bunch of people with a common interest who share what they've learned and consult each other to handle perplexing problems. It is one of the best forms of Mental Leverage because you can draw upon the resources of many other people sharing your interests.

Not long after personal computers began to be popular, Arthur V. bought one with no knowledge of how to use it.

"The instruction book told how to turn it on and check it out, but that was about it," Art recalls. "I could have taken some night courses on computing, but they were too general. What I needed was help in getting my brand of computer up and running and doing things for me."

Art formed a Mutual Interest Group. He went back to the store where he bought the computer and obtained the names of everyone who had purchased the same machine. Then he got in touch with each of them and suggested they get together.

"The response was terrific," Art says. "Most of the people had the same hunger as I for contact with other owners of that machine. A bunch of us got together, and we've been doing it once a month ever since. I tell you, I never would have been able to learn so much about using my computer without their help."

It isn't the only computer-related MIN that Art belongs to. After he learned how to operate his computer, he began thinking about having it programmed to help him pick investment stocks. He wrote a few simple investment programs, and then realized that he was probably reinventing the wheel.

"It struck me that other computer hobbyists all over the country must have been writing investment programs of their own," Art says, "and I was proven right when I saw a small announcement in a computer magazine. It had been inserted by someone who, like me, wanted to be in contact with other investment programmers. Well, I wrote to him, and so did scores of others, and now we have an informal MIN, mailing programs back and forth to each other."

Has Art made any money with the investment programs he's obtained?

"That's beside the point," he says with a grin. "The point is that I've learned a lot."

THE TWO REQUIREMENTS FOR FORMING A MUTUAL INTEREST NETWORK

All you need to get your own MIN started are these two things:

1. The names and addresses of other potential members;
2. A means of being in touch with each other.

You've seen two examples of how each of these requirements has been met. Art got the names and addresses of other buyers of the same computer from the store where he bought his. The investment programmer who started a nationwide MIN got Art and others to write to him after he inserted the notice in the hobby magazine.

The MIN that Art formed meets at members' homes; that's their means of being in touch with each other. On the other hand, the investment programming MIN keeps its members in touch with each other by means of a monthly newsletter and the personal correspondence that is conducted among the various participants.

One of the members of the investment programming MIN, Sherwin R., has formed a MIN in his home city. This one deals with investing, but not computing. It's like a traditional investment club, except that the members do not pool anything but knowledge.

"We make our own individual investment decisions," Sherwin wrote me when I inquired about the MIN, "but we share the information we've obtained on various stock issues."

You may wonder about the reason for this type of MIN when so much research material on stocks is available from brokerage houses and investment advisory services.

"Sure, there's plenty of material available," Sherwin explains. "In fact, too much for the average person to digest. In our MIN, each of us specializes in one particular type of stock. We study that on our own, and then report what we've found when we get together for lunch twice a month."

If, for example, Sherwin studies utility issues, then he can spend most of his investment study time on just those issues, knowing that other members of the MIN will be looking into other stocks. As Sherwin says, it's up to each member to make his own investment decisions, but the members all do so from a more informed basis, thanks to their Mutual Interest Network.

How much has it helped them?

"Most of us have been able to perform considerably better than the stock averages and even many mutual funds," Sherwin reports.

THE NUMBER ONE ADVANTAGE OF NETWORKING

You've seen living examples of the two major forms of personal networks:

1. The Knowledge Network in which you maintain a private list of experts to consult as the need arises;
2. The Mutual Interest Network in which people with a common interest agree to share what they have learned and experienced.

Mental Leverage is at work in both of these network forms. Just as with every other technique outlined in this book, networking allows you to greatly expand your mental power. Many of the techniques in earlier chapters had you using your mental power to tap hidden inner resources; in this chapter, you're learning how to tap outside resources.

No one individual can ever possibly hope to learn all there is to know about a given subject, but, thanks to networking, you can *access* all the information you need, when you need it. The number one advantage of networking is this:

Whenever you need a particular piece of information or knowledge, you know where to obtain it on short notice.

If it's a Knowledge Network, you have compiled a written listing of practical experts; if it's a Mutual Interest Network, you have every other participant to call on. In either case, you have greatly multiplied the knowledge-resources available to you.

There is, after all, little real difference between possessing a lot of information and knowing how to obtain it on short notice. We've all met, and been impressed by, people who boast of being able to carry a tremendous amount of specialized information in their heads. But, as we learned from Albert Einstein and Henry Ford back in Chapter 2, it's far easier to remember where to get information than to memorize the information itself.

Einstein found there was no reason to clutter his brain with information that could easily be looked up in a reference book. Ford said that when he didn't know the answer to a particular question, he could easily find someone to get the information for him.

In a sense, you are like Einstein and Ford when you create a personal network. You may not expect to become a mathematical genius or to invent a top-selling car, but you can benefit from one of the major keys to their success: leveraging your own knowledge with that of others. You can use that leveraged knowledge to achieve your highest ambitions.

MAKE MENTAL LEVERAGE AN IMPORTANT PART OF YOUR LIFE

I'll be the first to admit that you've been presented with some startling new ideas in this book. Most people are not aware of the total power behind their own mental resources until they actually begin utilizing the techniques you've seen spelled out in these fourteen chapters. But, when they begin to experience their newfound mental powers, and the benefits these powers bring, they regret that they weren't introduced to Mental Leverage much sooner.

I'll also be the first to admit that no one can be expected to absorb all that this book has to impart in one reading. After all, it contains entirely new methods of thinking, reasoning, learning, and remembering.

Now that you've read it through, you've been introduced to the exciting mental powers and techniques that can be yours. The time has come to start using them. Each chapter of this book holds a self-contained explanation of a valuable Mental Leverage skill. Take these skills one by one and make them yours.

The principles of Mental Leverage are amplified by many examples to illustrate the way. Continue to use these principles and examples as your guide in the weeks, months, and years ahead, and you will acquire mental skills far beyond your present limits. You will truly be unleashing the miracles of your mind.

Index